Performance & Customizing
for
Motorcycle Cruisers

Timothy Remus

Published by:
Wolfgang Publications Inc.
1310 Sunny Slope Ln
Stillwater, MN 55082

First published in 2000 by Wolfgang Publications Inc., 1310 Sunny Slope Ln, Stillwater MN 55082

ISBN number: 1-929133-02-2

Printed and bound in the USA

Motorcycle Cruisers

Acknowledgements

You'd think after all this time hammerin' out technical books that it would get easier. Somehow the opposite seems to be true. Each book becomes more work than the one before, requiring assistance from a long list of people. This particular book required trips to a variety of rallies, including Daytona and the Honda Hoot in Asheville, North Carolina (it's a tough job but….).

Thus I should start by thanking the Honda staff for inviting me to the Hoot, which is in fact pretty much of a good time and a great opportunity to see lots of bikes, bike owners and manufacturers. In fact, all the OEMs took time to help me with facts, figures and ideas on what the book should and shouldn't cover.

A few people within the industry need to be singled out. One is Jeff Palhegyi, who designs beautiful bikes for Yamaha and always took time to discuss bikes and send any material that I needed. In the aftermarket I need to thank Cory and Arlen Ness for helping with shop sequences, consenting to an interview, and for being generally hospitable. Blaine Birchfield from Cobra should get an award for having a consistently great attitude and a willingness to help. Dave Rollins from Thunder is another individual who provided a wealth of information of great value to most cruiser riders, all done with no strings attached. For advice on suspension I must thank Larry Langley at Progressive Suspension, while for help with billet wheel information I'm indebted to Pierre Elliott from Diamond Distributing.

John Zbiegien from JAZ Cycle provided more than information. John nearly gave me the keys to his shop so I could be sure to get exactly the photos I needed.

A couple of magazine editors helped as well. Evans Brasfield from *Motorcycle Cruiser* provided direction early in the project while Laura Brengelman from *Motorcycle Tour & Cruiser* shared with me some of her abundant good ideas and even better energy.

There's also a large group of people from all the other companies in the cruiser aftermarket who helped with ideas, information and images. These include Rhonda at Planet Cruiser, and the staff at PM, Aeromach and Küryakyn.

For layout I'm grateful to Joe Plumbo and Mike Urseth.

In closing I have to thank my lovely and talented wife Mary, who doesn't see much of me during the final two weeks before the book hits the press.

Introduction

Though cruiser bikes were for many years a relatively small part of the motorcycling market, today they command center stage. Anyone who doubts the importance of this market hasn't been to a dealer's show room or the manufacturers' tents in Daytona. Further proof can be found if you consider the vast amount of R&D that it takes to produce a complete line of "Star" bikes, a heavy hitting cruiser like the Victory (or the VTX Honda), or the really complete line of accessories from Kawasaki or Yamaha.

What it is:

This book is designed to answer a need. The need of cruiser riders for information. No one can leave their motorcycle alone, especially a cruiser bike. Meant for modification these bikes beg for just a little more chrome, some nice pinstripes and a bit more power.

This book is intended to help you improve both the performance and the looks of that cruiser in the driveway. Chapters on engine hop up, suspension improvements and brakes provide hard information on how those systems work and the best way to make them work better. The fastener chapter will help you bolt all those new parts in place.

Most riders approach the bike as a whole. That is, they don't just want a bike that's faster, they want one that's faster and has that certain custom look. For help in the looks department we've provided chapters on paint, design, and accessories. Interviews with Arlen Ness and Jeff Palhegyi provide a chance for amateurs to learn first-hand from professional bike builders.

What it's not

Despite all the technical information we've tried to cram into these pages, this is not a service manual. Because of what it's not, you need to buy a good manual for your particular bike. That way you have all the specifications for your particular machine, including things like the torque settings for all the nuts and bolts.

What you need

Most of the work involved in customizing a cruiser doesn't require great mechanical skills. You do need a set of tools and some basic mechanical ability. The two skills that most professional bike builders exhibit is great attention to detail, and the ability to see when something fits in the aesthetic sense. So perhaps what you really need to build that new bike is patience, a willingness to learn and the guts to simply give it a try.

Chapter One

Planning and Design

The most important part of the project

Whether your motorcycle project is a complete make-over or just a simple update with a few accessories and some suspension work, it pays to think first and buy parts second. The more money and time you intend to spend the more important it is that you plan out the changes, be they mechanical or aesthetic, so you are sure to achieve your goals.

Regardless the bike or budget, there are three over-riding goals that probably apply to this project: First, you want to make the bike your own, a

The more involved the project, the more important the planning becomes. Radical rides like this require careful thought so everything fits and the project turns out the way it was supposed to.

reflection of your tastes and personality. Second, you should strive to make it more fun to ride. Third, you need to make it at least as safe to ride and operate as it was stock.

First Things First

Before you begin planning out changes to the bike you've got to be brutally honest with yourself. You need to ask yourself: how much money do you have to spend, can you really do it all yourself, and what is the timeline - how long do you want it to be in pieces? The other piece of self-knowledge you need to possess before starting the project is just as important as the three items listed above: How do you intend to use the bike? Will it be a cruiser, a stoplight racer, or a show bike? (For more on this process of design check out the hints in Chapter Eight, Styling Ideas.)

Lying to yourself about the budget, especially if you're doing a lot of work to the bike, will only result in a machine that doesn't get finished. Or a bike that turns out half-fast because you had to skimp on materials at the end of the project. Closely related to the money issue is the matter of time and skill. How much work you send out to other people depends primarily on our own resume' of mechanical and creative skills.

In the case of a complete make-over it's important to allow enough time to do the project correctly. This will ensure that you don't have to stay up all night to get it finished before the show. More important, allowing enough time means you won't have to hassle the painter or chrome shop to get your stuff done NOW. Consider also the busy and slack periods most painters and specialty shops have, determined both by the season and the date of the next big run. Painters in Minnesota

The engine provides the spark that makes the bike what it is, in this case a very cool custom Road Star.

One of the first things most riders change is the exhaust. Choose yours to improve both the performance and the looks of the machine. Planet Cruiser

complain that people park the bike in October or November, but don't bring the sheet metal in until it's one week before Daytona

AESTHETIC CHANGES

Customizing your bike can be as simple as a new paint job or as complex as a compete disassembly and rebuild. Though it seems the fancy bikes with lots of expensive parts get all the attention in the magazines, there are plenty of killer machines built on a budget. If you want good visual impact plan the bike careful-

In this case, continuity in the design includes the entire bike, even the helmets.

Note the abundant chrome, which includes the wheels, fork bullets, calipers and a variet of grilles and covers.

ly. Understand that each parts affects and is affected by all the others. As my bike-building friend Jerry Berryhill from Little Rock likes to say: "Before selecting a part I ask: will it perform and will it match the rest of what I'm doing? There are guys here who've bought thousands of dollars worth of parts and they still end up with a bike that looks like the worst conglomeration of parts you've ever seen."

A major part of this planning should include the paint job. Don't just say, "I'm going to paint it black (or green or whatever) because I like black bikes." The paint job you chose is probably the most important single decision you will make regarding the overall look of the bike.

Most readers will simply paint the stock sheet metal and leave the frame alone. This means that in most cases you have to pick a paint color or scheme that works with the black frame. Those building a radical bike will want to pull the bike all the way down and paint the bare frame. Understand however, that pulling the bike down to a bare frame makes the project *much* more involved in terms of both time and money.

The easiest way to get it done is to simply pull

off the existing sheet metal and haul the parts down to the local painter. Consider that many of the new bikes come in one solid color, a perfect canvas for some tasteful pinstriping or graphics that can be done without removing the sheet metal.

Throughout this chapter, the Dream Bikes Chapter and the Styling Chapter we've tried to illustrate good simple design ideas. These example bikes and ideas cover a lot of ground, both in terms of money spent and in the type of bike they represent. Ultimately they are intended to highlight clever ideas and to make you think.

BIKE DESIGN 101

If you're planning a major building project it might be wise to follow the advice offered by many professional shops. Before undertaking a major project, most shops send the prospective customer home with a stack of bike magazines and instructions to mark all the bikes they really like. Maybe you already have a file of snap shots taken at the shows. Pull out the bikes that you most admire and try to decide what it is about those bikes that really appeals to you.

Working from your own photo or those in the magazines, you eventually need a picture or detailed sketch of what you want the new bike to look like, especially if you're stripping the bike to

Even a small cruiser can be personalized with the addition of a little paint work and some nice accessories. Smaller bikes can be harder to customized though because there aren't as many parts available.

The safest bet is to keep the changes to a dull roar. Start with a good looking bike, add things like exhaust, seat, bars and paint that appeal to your sense of design, and know when to say when. Cobra

Designer Jeff Palhegyi started the Desperado project by making "cool 18 inch spoked rims for a shaft drive cruiser." The bike also includes a hand-formed headlight nacelle, custom seat rail and fenders for what Jeff calls the "classic cruiser look." Dave Bush

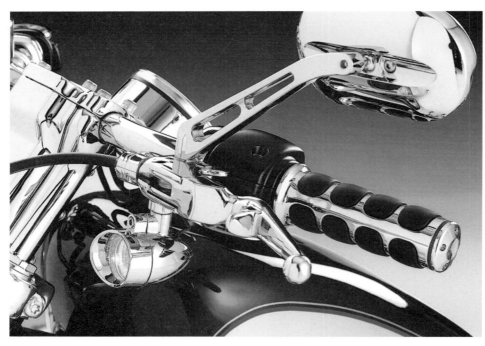

Small details make a big difference on a motorcycle. The bars, mirrors, grips and lighting all need to reflect your tastes and work together to complement the rest of the bike. Küryakyn

the frame and starting over. Though it might be tempting to just pull the bike apart and be spontaneous, it's dangerous to "let it happen." You need plans and sketches, not a five thousand dollar surprise.

Experienced builders often start with a photo of a bike similar to the one they want to build. At the local copy and printing store they make big black and white blow-ups of the photo. Now they can "customize" the bike with scissors and glue. A different fork rake is just a matter of cut and paste. A new color can be had simply by purchasing some colored markers. Cut, paste and then make more copies. This is a cheap way to visualize and finalize your plans for the new bike. You can also start with a photo of your existing bike, scan it into the computer, and then use a program like PhotoShop to do the "customizing." All without turning a wrench.

Whether you use a simple sketch or a sophisticated rendering, it's important to know ahead of time what the new bike will look like. Keep the image of the new bike taped to the tool box, it will keep you focused on the project and prevent your being distracted when a new fad blows into town.

For anyone doing extensive work with new sheet metal on hand, the mock-up stage is very useful. Professional builders mock up the bike before final assembly and before the paint is applied. They set the bare bike on the hoist and clamp on the new fenders, tank and wheels. This way they know for sure that all the parts fit the bike and where any necessary holes should be drilled.

This is a good time to look over the bike to ensure the parts fit in a design or aesthetic sense. To get a proper look at the bike it should be up off the floor in a shop that's big enough so you can actually get back to really "see" the bike the way it's going to look on the street. Some builders roll the mock-up outside and then look it over from various angles.

Sometimes a slight change in the position or angle of a fender makes a tremendous difference in the way a machine looks. The mock up stage is a good time to double check the good-looks of your new design. If you think a different fender might look better than the one you've chosen, borrow one and clamp it in place. Don't send the parts out for paint and plating until you're happy with the overall look of the bike.

Copper Classic is another Royal Star built by Jeff Palhegyi. The big Yamaha uses long fenders and wide bars to create what Jeff calls "the beach cruiser look." Dave Bush

ENGINE AND MECHANICAL CHANGES

Much like aesthetic changes, changes and improvements to the engine's performance should be made only after you've done some home-work. Read the Engine Chapter in this book. When you go to a show, find other riders with bikes

This project Kawasaki from PM utilizes their wheels, rotors and calipers, combined with aftermarket fenders, lights and exhaust.

like yours. What have they done to the bike and are they happy with the results? Most cruiser engines have an untapped reserve of power. If what you want is "another ten horsepower," that can usually be had without major engine work.

Before doing engine work ask yourself what you want the bike to do. The more you want from the engine the more important the planning phase becomes. Because this is Book One, we've elected to stay with fairly simple engine

Kenny Keen's Kawasaki started out as a Nomad. He decided to try a "new look." Thus the Kawi bags have been replaced with leather bags from H-D.

upgrades. If what you're trying to do is beat your buddy's ZX-11, you need to do some *serious* homework. Part of that homework is finding the right shop to do the engine work.

When doing any king of engine upgrade avoid the allure of the silver bullet. That one magic carburetor or set of exhaust pipes that *by themselves*, will yield a huge increase in horsepower and torque. Significant increases in power usually come about through the careful installation of a package of parts.

This book focuses on mild engine hop ups. Situations where the installation of a jet kit, air filter and/or pipes will yield useful gains in horsepower and torque. All without giving up longevity or tractability on the street. These are situations where a modest expenditure of cash can bring about substantial increases in power.

Whether the project involves a mechanical upgrade or a visual change (often both) the important thing is to think your way through – before getting out the wrenches. Because the more you think about this bike-building project and the more you plan, the more likely you are to succeed.

The bike uses Dunlop white-wall tires in stock sizes, mounted to billet rims from Diamond Distributing. A spring kit in the front fork and a pair of 12-1/2 inch Progressive shocks lower the bike two inches.

ARLEN NESS INTERVIEW

When it comes time to fix up that cruiser, the first issue to be discussed isn't paint color or which seat to buy. The first issue is the issue of money.

In order to provide some customizing ideas, placed within a real-world context, we asked the world's best known motorcycle designer, Arlen Ness, for his ideas categorized by budget.

So if you need help deciding what to do with a limited budget. Or what to do first, second and third, read on as Arlen shares with us what he's learned in over thirty years of transforming two wheelers from boring to beautiful.

Arlen, considering that not everyone has the same budget, let's look at the best way to spend some money fixing up a Metric cruiser. From an aesthetic standpoint what's the best way to spend the following approximate amounts, not including labor for installation of any parts?

(Note: each amount listed is the total amount spent, i.e., at the $1500 level you're spending an *additional* $1000.00.)

$500.00

For five hundred bucks I probably would want to change the mufflers, that would be the first thing I'd do. Install some slip-ons if I could, or a complete exhaust, to get the bike to sound good. Then I would rejet the carb or add a chip if it's a fuel injected bike, whatever you have to do to make it run good with those pipes.

A good design study. Under the sheet metal and paint most of these are the same motorcycle.

All cruisers don't have to look alike. Used in the Planet Cruiser catalog, Speedstar exhibits some very European design influences, including the unusual rear fender and struts, the trim front fender, and European forks.

The nice thing about the current state of cruisers is the wealth of material the aftermarket offers. This means you can easily add accents that match each other and your intentions for the bike. Cobra

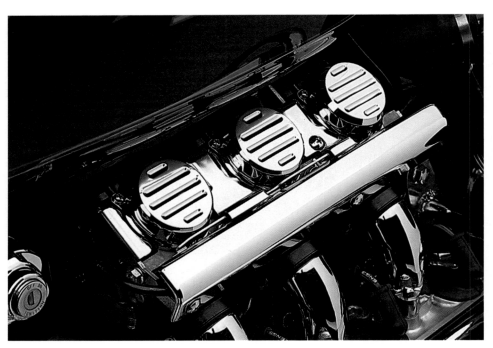

These "milled" carburetor covers are just one example of a complete line of accessories, all with the same design and finish. Cobra

Now it sounds better and runs better too. Good performance is so important, especially in California because the stock bikes never run very well here. **$1500.00**

Now I would lower the bike, front and rear. Then I would change the bars and probably add a new seat. If I had money left over the next thing would be new grips and mirrors, they're really part of the bars. **$2500.00**

With this much money I would change the fenders, especially the rear fender, they're always mounted too high from the factory. But sometimes when people put on a fender they don't get it to follow the rim. The fender ends up too high in the back or they roll it around too far. When putting on a fender they need to stand back and really look at it and get it right.

The new fender (which needs to be painted) will make the bike look a lot zoomier. And I might add a license plate bracket and a new taillight assembly at the same time. **$5000.00**

With the extra $2500 I would go to wheels and brakes, maybe an eighteen inch wheel in the rear and a nineteen or twenty one in front. The wheels and brakes, they really make a motorcycle. At this point it would be nice to have some paint and graphics too.

This would be a pretty nice looking bike. It's lowered, has a nice seat, the good wheels and brakes, and some paint or graphics.

For five grand you would have a pretty slick looking motorcycle.

Arlen, in closing, do you want to talk a little bit about the mistakes people make when they fix up their bikes. Places where they don't spend their money wisely.

People go and they buy a new bike, the Harley guys do this, and then they buy all that live-to-ride stuff from the dealer. And they put all that on the bike. Then they go to their first couple of events and see some good stuff. Now they throw away all the accessories they bought at first and start over. They buy it all twice. I tell them to wait a little bit until they know what they want so they only buy it once.

Proof that there's no limit to what you can do with a "metric" cruiser comes in the form of this stretched Victory bagger from Arlen Ness. Mike Chase Photo Design

A motorcycle designer for over thirty years, Arlen Ness is currently working on designs and ideas for Victory, Kawasaki and Yamaha motorcycles.

With or without the small fairing, the Victory exhibits that certain classic look. Note the spoked wheels with polished rims, stretched gas tank and long fenders. Mike Chase Photo Design

Chapter Two

Engine Performance Upgrades

Lookin' for easy Horsepower

Most cruiser riders are looking for a little more horsepower. As luck would have it, the cruiser bikes they buy come with engines in a mild state of tune. These engines might be said to have unrealized potential, or untapped reserves or power and torque. So the trick here is to unleash the ponies hiding inside the engine cases.

Though you can build an engine from mild to wild, the intent of this book is to look for the easiest, safest way to add horsepower and torque without giving up the engine's ability to work on the street as an everyday rider. For the most part we've

Motorcycle engines are different that car engines - they're hanging' out there for all to see. Your engine "hop up" should include more than just extra horsepower.

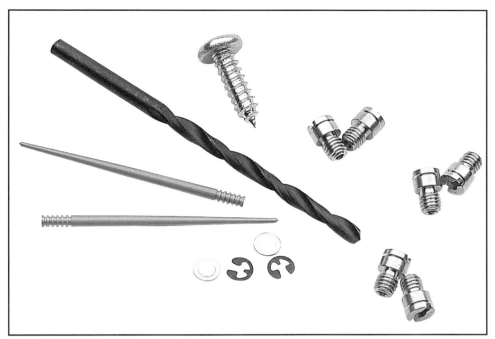

Most jet kits include a main jet, tapered needle and pilot jet. The drill and screw make it easy to remove the cap that covers the idle mixture screw.

the factory. Obtaining more horsepower, and often better mileage as well, from these engines is generally a matter of changing the air box, the pipes and rejetting the carburetor.

As Dave Rollins from Thunder explains in the interview farther along in this chapter, another ten horsepower can be had with relative ease from most modern cruisers. The recipe he outlines is pretty straightforward. Give the engine more air, ensure the waste products from each power stroke are

avoided the discussion of high compression pistons and new camshafts with wild profiles that don't "turn on" until you've reached 4000 RPM.

The idea is to help you add horsepower and torque in the low to mid-range where most of us ride most of the time All this without giving up reliability and mileage (though there may be some trade-offs).

In an effort to bring to bear some real-life examples, we've tapped the database at JAZ cycle, a small shop run by John Zbiegien Jr. At Jaz they've done a number of mild hop ups, and documented the increases with careful before and after dyno runs. As you will see by reading through the results in the In The Shop section, significant power increases can be yours without tearing apart the engine or installing a Nitrous injection kit.

For additional information on the best way to find those "easy horses" we also present an interview with Dave at Thunder Motorcycle Accessories.

A LITTLE MORE POWER

We all want just a little more power. Enough to beat our buddy in the other lane. Enough to provide a little rush when you whack the throttle open. As we've already said, most cruisers come to market with V-Twin engines that are very mildly tuned by

Air kits like this, available in many styles for most cruisers, include everything you need to add an extra dose of oxygen on each intake stroke. Thunder Mfg.

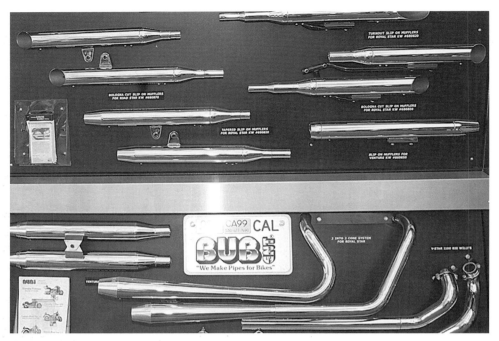

A large number of firms now manufacture exhaust systems and slip-on mufflers for the cruiser market, making it much easier to find just the right blend of looks and performance.

This two-into-one system combines classic looks with the inherent advantages of this design. Also available with smooth heat shields. Roadhouse

encouraged to fully vacate the cylinder during the exhaust stroke and then provide more fuel to so the mixture doesn't go too lean. In order to better understand this common hop up practice it might help to examine each part of the process.

THE AIR BOX

In this market what many of us grew up calling an air filter is often referred to as an air box. The name makes sense because the bikes don't necessarily mount a chrome air cleaner right in front of the carburetor. On the big Kawasakis for example, what looks like an air cleaner on the right side is really just a big chamber.

Whether the factories do it to "tune" the engine or to muffle the sound of the intake roar, many cruisers use a complicated intake air tract leading up to the carburetor. The Kawasaki Vulcan pulls air from under the tank, routes it to the left where the air filter is, then through a crossover tube to the other side of the engine, through the big "air cleaner" on the right side and finally to the carburetor. It's not too surprising that more power can be had simply by eliminating all the plumbing leading up to the carburetor throat.

A growing number of companies offer replacement kits that eliminate the factory air box or air cleaner with a straight forward air cleaner equipped with a low restriction and reusable air filter from a company like K&N.

In buying an air box kit you need to find a design that you find aesthetically pleasing from a company with a good track record. This is another case where it helps to ask riders of bikes like yours what their experience has been with Company X, Y or Z. Does the air cleaner they offer make more power? Is it easy to install? Does the company offer tech advice like which jets to install to get the carburetor back to the correct air fuel ratio? It's also helpful to spend some time with the various vendors at a big rally like the Honda Hoot or Daytona. This provides a good opportunity to compare the relative quality of the products from different companies while listening to each vendor's sales pitch.

EXHAUST

Very likely the first thing most riders do to their bikes is change the exhaust. The decision is a no-brainer. The default setting. Better looks, more power and a more pleasing sound all await the buyer who steps up and installs an exhaust system.

There are as many styles and manufacturers of aftermarket pipes as there are cruiser models. There are the always-popular drag pipes, and slash-cut drag pipes and probably about six more types of drag pipes. Drag as in drag race, and indeed these pipes do work well on an all-out competition machine. The problem is, most engines run better around town with some restriction in the exhaust pipes, especially when each cylinder has it's own exhaust pipe. Most engine tuners report that drag pipes don't make good mid-range power and they have trouble with transitions from one speed to another. If you really like the looks of drag, or straight, pipes, then buy a set with baffles.

For the same reasons, the really fat pipes of two inches or more may not be the most powerful. Some companies have come up with designs that let you have your cake and eat it too. These huge pipes are actually a chrome cover over a smaller exhaust

The manufacturers' displays at the big rallys often include displays like this one, which make it much easier to compare the various exhaust systems.

You don't always have to replace the entire exhaust system. Better looks and improved performance can often be had with a pair of slip on mufflers like these. Cobra

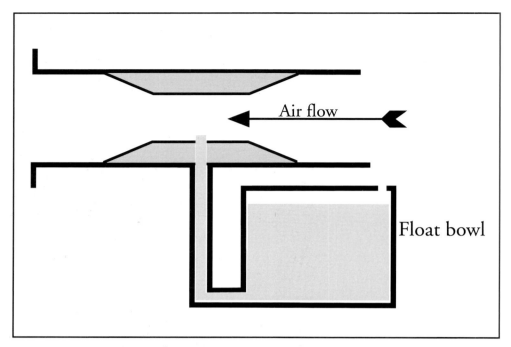

Air flow

Float bowl

At the heart of every carburetor is a venturi, a restriction in the pipe. Air pressure within the venturi is reduced, so gas (under atmospheric pressure) flows to the venturi where is is atomized and mixed with air.

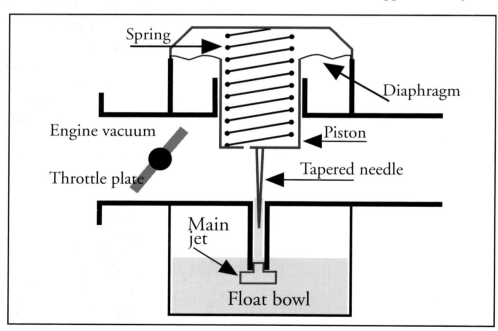

Spring

Diaphragm

Engine vacuum

Piston

Throttle plate

Tapered needle

Main jet

Float bowl

A CV carburetor uses a floating piston to create a variable venturi the size of which is determined by engine speed and load. Higher speeds create increased vacuum which works against the spring to open the venturi. As the piston moves up the tapered needle is pulled farther out of the orifice - providing more fuel.

pipe. The covers are also a nice way to eliminate any blueing of the pipe.

Staggered duals might qualify as the next most popular pipe on the market. Again sold in a wide variety of styles and lengths, most of these have a small muffler near the end of each individual pipe. Some allow you to change tips or muffler assemblies to achieve a different look.

Two-into-one pipes are known for their good mid-range power delivery. The problem is most riders prefer a more traditional exhaust system. A little harder to find as well, Cobra, Bub, Roadhouse, Vance & Hines as well as a few others make these efficient exhaust systems for most of the big cruiser models.

Duals. Even the word conjures up images of chopped Mercury leadsleds and hopped up '55 Chevys. Not the exhaust for every situation, a set of duals somehow looks "right" on most dressers and touring rigs. One of the nice things about duals is the fact that these systems mount the mufflers low enough to clear the bottom of the saddle bag.

ALTERNATIVES

In some cases you can simply install new mufflers. Something that will "slip on" the existing exhaust pipe. It's an easy and less expensive way to get the sound and looks you're after.

When it comes time to install that new exhaust system John Zbiegien from JAZ Cycle explains that people have trouble, "because they want to tighten the pipes up at the cylinder head right away, and then the guy can't get them to hang right at the back or fit the brackets." You have to hang the whole exhaust system on loosely, then when you know everything is going to fit you can tighten up the flange nuts evenly. Then when the flanges are tight the remaining mounting bolts can be tightened up.

NOISE

It seems only fair to make a short statement about what comes out the end of the exhaust pipes. Not the carbon monoxide, but rather the sound. The catalogs advertise pipes with a "mellow" sound. A drag pipe is anything but mellow, especially under full throttle at 4500 RPM.

We all love the sound of a V-Twin, that's why we ride the damned things. But if a little is good a lot isn't necessary better, or faster. Among the loudest of the pipes are the drag pipes and many of the staggered duals. Harley guys say that Loud Pipes Save Lives. My friend Michael, a rider for many years, says Loud Pipes Cause Helmet Laws. Translation: when you piss off the people in every car or house you pass you've created a lot of potential enemies when a anti-motorcycling bill comes up in the state legislature. Think a little about noise and neighbors and real-world power before deciding which exhaust system to buy.

THE CARBURETOR

A good carburetor supplies a regulated quantity of air and fuel to the engine at all times. No matter how hot or cold the engine is or how quickly you whack open the throttle, the engine will receive the correct amount of fuel for optimum operation.

At the heart of nearly any carburetor is a venturi, or a restriction of some kind in the carburetor throat. When you force air through a restriction in a pipe the speed of the air increases as it moves through the restriction. As the velocity goes up the pressure goes down. Now if we introduce gasoline at this low pressure point in the venturi, subject to atmospheric pressure at the other end, the gas will be "pushed" out into the air-stream where it can atomize and mix with the air on its way to the cylinders.

A simple carburetor like that described above might work on a constant speed engine. On the street we need a means of controlling the flow of air

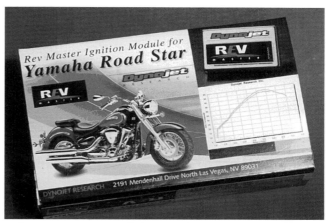

This Rev Master is the unit John used on the Road Star to increase the rev limit from 4200 to a more reasonable 5000 RPM.

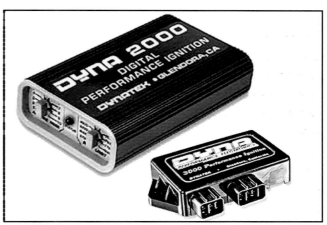

Each Dyna ignition includes a number of pre-mapped ignition curves, one of which is sure to match your particular combination of engine improvements.

Among the many exhaust systems available are these straight pipes available for most cruisers. Jardine

Seen during installation on a Road Star, the Hypercharger provides better breathing for your favorite V-twin and a ram-air effect at higher speeds.

through the carburetor along with some extra fuel circuits.

Carburetors are designed to work in three conditions: idle, low speed (mid-range) and high speed. Most carburetors have these three basic circuits, plus some additional circuits to ease the transition from one condition to another. Real-world carburetors have to deal with situations like cold starts and sudden acceleration. A cold engine needs an extra-rich mixture for example, because gas doesn't like to atomize with cold air. Sudden acceleration, on the other hand, means the amount of air passing down the throat of the carburetor increases instantly, while the heavier fuel takes considerably longer to catch up. So we add a choke or enrichment circuit for cold starts and an accelerator pump, (not all carbs have one) to squirt a little extra gas down the carb throat when you suddenly open the throttle.

Motorcycles commonly use three types of carburetor: constant velocity, slide and butterfly. Because the most common carburetor in the cruiser-land is the CV, we will run through a brief description of that design and a short explanation of which components are commonly changed to recalibrate the carburetor after the rider changes the exhaust or air box.

CONSTANT VELOCITY CARBURETORS

In a CV carb the throttle cable is connected to a conventional butterfly valve. Upstream from the butterfly valve is the variable restriction in the carburetor throat. This restriction is held in the closed position by a spring and opens according to vacuum within the carb throat. More vacuum causes the piston to open farther, increasing the size of the venturi. At idle both the butterfly and the venturi are closed. As the throttle is opened more vacuum is applied to the slide piston, the piston moves up until

Serious horsepower, as much as twice the stock output, can be had with the installation of a turbo kit from Mr. Turbo. The installation is so neat no one knows the turbo is there until you twist the grip. Kawasaki

equilibrium is achieved between the spring pushing down and the vacuum pulling up. During all this up and down movement of the piston, the velocity of air through the carburetor throat stays constant, thus the name.

One of the claimed advantages of the CV design is the fact that if you open the throttle right off idle, at a time when the engine may not really be ready for that much air, the CV carb only delivers as much air (along with the correct amount of fuel) as the engine can use at that speed. As RPMs increase the slide moves up allowing more and more air to pass down the carburetor throat. The farther the slide moves up the farther the tapered needle is pulled out of the orifice, which effectively increases the size in a nice seamless fashion.

Going back to the three basic circuits inside each carburetor. Most CV carbs use a pilot jet to control the low speed, the main jet to control high speed and the tapered needle to handle the situations between. Most "jet kits" or recalibration kits sold for metric bikes with CV carburetors include one or more main and pilot jets, as well as a new needle. For a look at the actual process of rejetting a CV carburetor check out the In The Shop sequence in this chapter.

IGNITION

As stated, most cruiser owners who want more power without tearing apart the engine add an air box kit, a new set of pipes and a jet

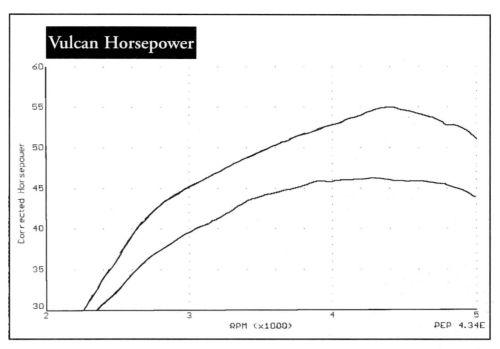

The before and after horsepower chart for the Shop-time Vulcan on page. 24 shows an increase of nine horsepower, not bad for a series of mild modifications. The best part though is the fact that the extra power starts low in the RPM range and just builds all the way to redline.

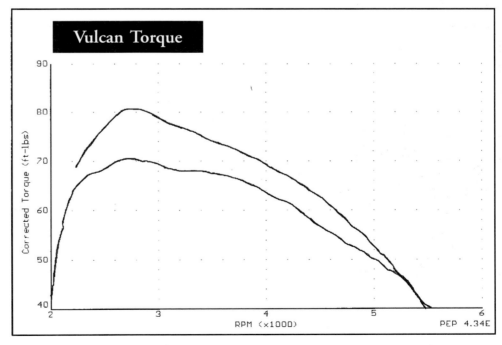

We all talk about horsepower but it's torque that gets the job done. In the case of the Vulcan we've added eleven foot pounds and like the horsepower gains, the extra torque is available low in the RPM range.

Shop Time: Engine Hop Up

For a look into the real-world of mild engine hop ups, we spent a few days at JAZ Cycle Service in Spring Lake Park, Minnesota. Jaz does a wide range of work on mostly metric motorcycles. The sequence documented here covers the work done to a Kawasaki 1500 Vulcan Classic.

TEST CASE #1

The addition of a Hypercharger, carburetor recalibration kit, and new exhaust to a Kawasaki Vulcan 1500.

Like most modern V-Twin cruisers the big

The finished Vulcan, with Samson pipes, Hypercharger and a rejetted carb. This bike has another Hypercharger on the other side.

After removing the small dash cluster. the rest of the dash can be removed, followed by the front hold-down bolt.

Vulcan suffers from a lack of oxygen. Despite the 1500cc displacement the big Kawi only puts out about 50 horsepower. Documented here is the transformation of one stock Vulcan 1500 from mild to mildly-wild. With the addition of a Hypercharger (actually two Hyperchargers, but we'll get to that in a minute) and some additional work, this 1998 Vulcan went from 46 horsepower and 69 foot pounds of torque, to 55 horses and 80 foot pounds of torque.

GETTING DOWN TO WORK

The work starts in the Jaz Cycle Service shop where John Zbiegien rips the Kawasaki apart before beginning the task of unleashing the horses hidden within the black cases and cylinders. First to come off is the forward part of the seat, followed by the small dash cluster. Removing the dash means first taking out the screws that hold it to the tank, then lifting it up to unhook the three wiring plugs underneath and the speedometer cable.

With the dash off John can remove the gas tank attaching bolt under the dash, and the other one at the tail end of the tank near the seat. Before lifting the tank John turns off the petcock and takes the gas line off at the petcock. There are also two small drain tubes that John disconnects at the tank.

If you decide to duplicate this work at home, remember that gasoline is extremely flammable. It's a good idea to disconnect the battery before starting the work to eliminate the chance that you might create a spark while working on the bike. John drains gas from the lines and the float bowl into a small, clean can and then puts that back in the tank. He also keeps a rag nearby that is used to absorb any small gas dribbles from the carburetor or the lines while he's working on the bike. Don't let this rag sit in the corner with other rags when you're done with the work or it could start a fire by spontaneous combustion.

Once the seat and tank are off John can take the complete air box assembly off the bike. The

Shop Time: Engine Hop Up

The rear hold-down bolt is one of two that hold the tank to the frame.

To take the choke cable and knob out of the bracket the nut on the back side must be loosened first.

Now the tank can be lifted up, so hoses underneath can be disconnected.

This is the bracket that will be used later to support the adapter for the Hyper charger.

With the carb lifted up and out of the way, John can pull the cross-over air tube out of the way.

The gas line must be disconnected where it connects to the carburetor.

Shop Time: Engine Hop Up

These anti freeze hoses are hard to remove, making it easier to leave the carb hanging on the bike

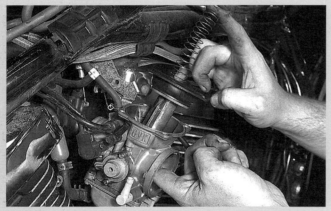

With the cover off the top of the carb, John can remove the CV slide and the spring that helps to determine the position of the slide.

The tapered needle, one of the parts that is changed during this "rejetting," mounts into the center of the slide.

stock Kawasaki draws air from under the gas tank then to the left side where it is filtered before being routed through a tube to the right side "air cleaner" and eventually to the carburetor through a rubber hose. One look at this convoluted stock air box it's easy to believe that replacing it will result in better breathing and more power.

Removing the air box means taking off the long air-tube that runs under the carburetor and the separate section that bolts into place under the bottom of the gas tank. To make it easier to remove the air tube that passes under the carb, John cuts off the two little plastic ears that protrude from the side of the tube. Trimming off the ears saves John the hassle of removing the intake manifold.

Now it's time to pull the carburetor off the manifold. On the big Kawasakis John leaves the carburetor hanging on the bike. As he explains, "The Kawasakis have two anti freeze hoses that go to the carb to heat it, and it's easier to just leave those hooked up to the carb and work on the carb as it hangs on the bike."

Disconnecting the carb from the intake manifold means loosening a clamp on the back side of the carburetor, accessed from above after the tank is removed. Before pulling the carb away from the manifold John also takes the idle speed knob out of its bracket on the right side, and the choke knob out of a similar bracket on the left side. The choke cable runs up and behind the rear cylinder on its way to the carburetor. It's very hard to actually remove from the bike so John pushes gently on the outer cable and slides some of it up toward the carb. This way there's enough slack in the cable that he can pull the carburetor away from the engine. The last two things to come off the carburetor before it's moved away from the engine are the vent hose on the top of the carb and the throttle cable bracket on the front of the carburetor (check the photos here to relieve confusion).

Once he can pull the carb away from the engine John disconnects the vacuum line leading

Shop Time: Engine Hop Up

The float bowl is removed next, though the accelerator pump linkage keeps it from being totally separated from the body of the carburetor.

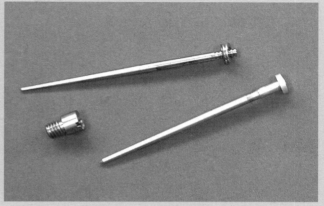

On the top, the replacement needle with grooves that allow fine-tuning of the position. On the bottom the stock needle and between them a main jet.

A small screw driver is used to remove the pilot or low speed jet seen here.

During reassembly, it's important that the vacuum diaphragm for the slide be correctly installed with the lip in the matching recess in the body of the carb.

And a bigger screw driver is used next to change the main jet.

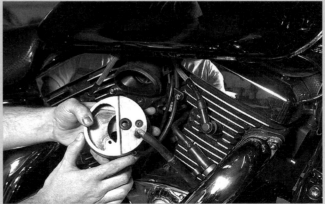

This is the backs side of the adapter for the Hypercharger, ready to mate up with the lip on the rubber hose connected to the carburetor.

Shop Time: Engine Hop Up

Installation of a Hypercharger on this Vulcan means first installing the adapter.....

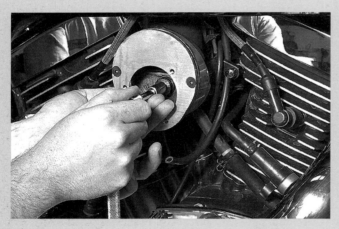

.... which is bolted to the bracket seen earlier that stretches between the two cylinders.

Now the vacuum hose is hooked up and the 'charger is bolted to the adapter. All that's left is the cover.

to the carb. This line will in fact be cut and "T-ed" as the vacuum source for the Hypercharger.

Now John can carefully pull the top carb cover off (there's a spring underneath so it wants to spring up and out of the way.) Per the instructions that come with the Küryakyn recalibration kit he removes the diaphragm and slide. Next, he carefully drills out the hole in the slide piston, and replaces the factory tapered needle with the one provided in the kit. (This is all covered in the instructions that come with the recalibration kit.) When reinstalling the diaphragm it's important that the lip be seated at the edge of the carb and that there be no tears of holes in the diaphragm itself.

Next, John pulls off the float bowl. With the four screws out, John pulls the bowl away from the body of the carb and carefully dumps the gas onto a rag so it doesn't run all over the engine and the floor.

The float bowl is swung out of the way, but is left attached to the rest of the carb by the accelerator pump linkage. Now John uses a thin straight-blade screwdriver to remove the stock pilot jet (also known as the low-speed jet) and replace it with the number 48 jet supplied with the kit.

Next up for replacement is the main jet, the one hanging out there in the open with the float bowl off. The instructions recommend a number 135 main jet, (though bikes with certain low-restriction pipes might need one of the slightly larger jets provided, and those operated at higher elevations might need the slightly smaller 132 jet provided in the kit.) With these two jets replaced John can reinstall the float bowl, carefully working his way around the float bowl, tightening the four screws carefully in stages until all are nice and tight.

The final step before reassembly is to drill out the cover over the idle mixture screw, insert the sheet metal screw provided, and then "pop" the cover out of the way so the idle mixture screw can be adjusted later.

Shop Time: Engine Hop Up

Once the carburetor is reassembled and reinstalled on the intake manifold, John can use his own installation kit to install the Hypercharger from Küryakyn. The installation utilizes the stock rubber air snorkel between the carburetor and a Thunder Manufacturing billet adapter that mounts to the back side of the Hypercharger. The billet adapter, in turn, is supported by the original factory air cleaner support bracket that bolts between the two cylinders

With the billet adapter bolted in place John can now mount the Hypercharger to the adapter. Installing the Hypercharger means cutting the vacuum hose to the carb and installing a T fitting. This fitting is the source of vacuum that operates the flaps on the front of the air cleaner.

HYPERCHARGER NUMBER TWO

More and more cruiser owners are installing a second air cleaner to the bikes "other side" in order to give the bike balance. John has assembled a kit that makes it easy to install a second Hypercharger to the left side of this Kawasaki. The kit consists of a special bracket, the air manifold and a left side hyper charger with a set of instructions. In addition to the Hypercharger and recalibration kit, John also installed a pair of Samson long-shot pipes.

THE DYNO RUN: JOHN PUTS HIS MONEY WHERE HIS MOUNT IS

Anyone can talk about how fast their bike is or how much horsepower it has since they installed the Brand X air box kit or super-slash pipes or whatever. At JAZ cycle they like to do before and after dyno runs to show customers exactly how much the bike improved.

The Dyno is a model 200 from Dyna Jet, and each "run" consists of about 6 to 8 pulls on the dyno. In addition to checking total horsepower and torque, the dyno can be thought of as an elaborate road test, one more opportunity to make sure the bike runs as good as it can.

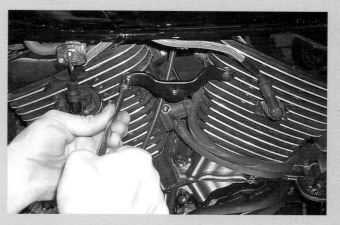

Installing a Hypercharger on the left is done by using the factory bracket and the kit from JAZ.

The left side 'charger or air cleaner is for looks only in most cases.

The proof is in the dyno run. The Kawasaki picked up eleven foot pounds and nine horsepower.

kit to the carburetor. Some go slightly beyond this basic recipe with a new ignition from a company like Dyna.

The advantage of a new ignition are two fold: first, the new ignition will generally provide more spark (more voltage) than the stock ignition, which can help to fire the plugs in a high compression engine or one that is run hard. The bigger advantage of a new ignition is the possibility of choosing a different ignition curve than that provided by the factory.

Many of the new ignition modules come with ten or more ignition curves. The manufacturer of the ignition module will generally provide advice as to which curve should be used with which combination of parts. A bike with an air box kit and a set of pipes might do well with curve number three or four, while an engine with high-compression pistons and more radical camshafts can benefit from curve number six or seven. Before buying a new ignition module in that quest for more power, be sure to check the claims and dyno charts from the manufacturer of the ignition so there are no surprises or disappointments.

We should mention that most stock ignitions have a rev limiter built in. Designed to shut off the engine at some reasonable level, like 5000 RPM, these limiters make sense. A few bikes however, like the Yamaha Road Star, have the rev limiter set at such a low level that they benefit greatly from a kit that will raise the ceiling from 4200 RPM (in the case of the Road Star) to some more reasonable level like 5000 or 5500 RPM. In this case the rev limiter is a separate electronic component that can be easily replaced by a new and more liberal limiter from the aftermarket.

PUTTING IT ALL TOGETHER – SOME REAL WORLD HOP UPS.

A set of pipes, or a new air box kit, will result in better breathing and more power for most V-twin cruisers. In the real world most riders do both, an exhaust system and an air box kit. This requires recalibration of the carburetor.

A Test Case

We though it would be interesting to present a documented set of improvements to a current cruiser. The bike presented here in abbreviated form is a Yamaha Road Star. (For a more detailed look at what it takes to get extra power from a Cruiser, check out the work done to a Kawasaki 1500 in the side-bar in this chapter.) The work on the Yamaha was done at JAZ Cycle Service, the same operation that did the work seen in the In The Shop sequence. The work done on the Yamaha is very similar to that done to the Kawasaki shown in the side-bar in this chapter, with one important difference.

Like the Kawasaki, the Yamaha received a Hypercharger kit, a recalibrated carburetor and a new set of pipes. The difference between the two approaches involves the ignition on the Yamaha. While the Kawi was left with stock ignition, the

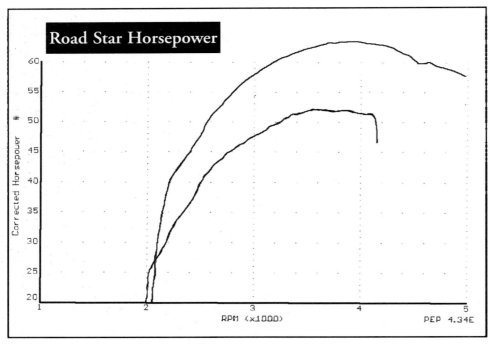

Another win-win situation, the Road Star gained twelve horses and much of that power is available as low as 2200 RPM. Because of the Rev Master the peak power doesn't suddenly disappear at 4200 RPM.

Yamaha received a new Rev Master module from Dyna. As John explains, "the trouble with the Yamaha is the rev limiter from the factory. These are set to 4200 RPM. So just about the time the bike is really starting to pull the engine shuts down. The new unit from Dyna raises the rev-ceiling to 5000 RPM."

The results

With the new Hypercharger to let more air in, the new exhaust to make sure the spent gasses have a way out, and the recalibrated carb and revised ignition, the Yamaha went from a stock reading of 52 horsepower and 85 foot pounds of torque to substantially better readings of 64 and 98 respectively. For other examples of real-world power increases check out the interview in this chapter.

INTERVIEW - DAVE ROLLINS AT THUNDER MOTORCYCLE ACCESSORIES

Dave, how about some background on you and Thunder.

I've been riding since 1965, I worked as a helicopter mechanic in the military, during Vietnam. Then after the service, in the early 1970s, I built choppers and I always worked on bikes for my friends. I started Thunder in 1997, out of my love for motorcycles and the need that I saw for cruiser parts. The market was growing and growing and nobody was doing anything. I kept waiting for someone to do something and nothing

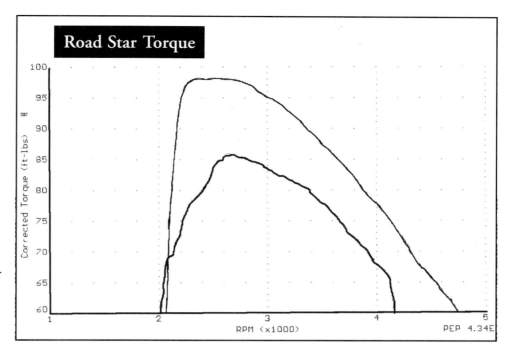

To say the changes yielded a dramatic increase in torque is an understatement. Note how quickly the torque reaches peak value with the modifications.

The finished Yamaha, with hypercharger, rejetted carb and straight pipes from Cobra.

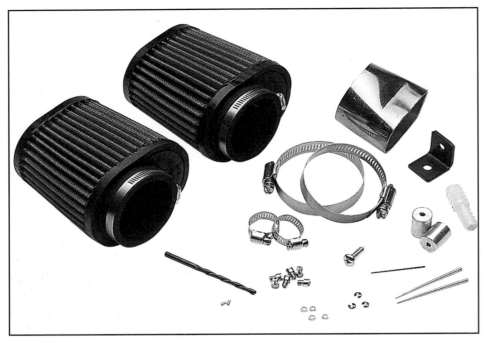

Some of the Vulcans came with an air filter hung on the right side of the bike just ahead of the gas tank. This kit eliminates the "add on" air filter and improves breathing. Cobra

Air box kits from Thunder come in a variety of styles, including this teardrop shape seen on a Kawasaki.

happened so I decided to fill the bill.

You do engine parts and cosmetic parts as well?

Yes, we do a few cosmetic things but most of what we do involves horsepower.

With most stock V-Twin cruiser bikes, is it relatively easy to get good increases in horsepower without disassembling the engine?

Yes, the first thing a person needs to realize is that all these motors are big air pumps. The more air you get in and out, the more power you make. The first five or ten or even fifteen horses come pretty easy by increasing the airflow.

Can you talk about what you recommend for a cruiser owner who wants more power but doesn't want to go so far as to add camshafts, high-compression pistons and all the rest.

I recommend an increase in the airflow, a new air filter system. Some people call it a new air box. When that is done you need to jet the carburetor for more airflow. What most people don't realize is that when you increase flow, you also need to reconfigure the fuel mixture. If you shove more air into it, it goes lean. Now you need to bring that fuel mixture back to between 13.5 and 13.8 parts air per one part of fuel. As you increase the amount of air, that doesn't mean the gas mileage will go down, typically it goes up.

Are most of the bikes the same? Does the same recipe work for all of the current V-Twin cruisers? What about the bikes with smaller engines and/or two carburetors?

The basic idea, again, is more air flow. So that basic recipe is the same for all of them. Twin carb bikes usually run better from the factory than single carb bikes but there are still gains to be made. The 750 and the 1100 Honda Shadows have twin carbs. They're a little different though we get eight additional horse power on the 1100. In fact we get an additional eight horse-power from the new 600 Honda.

Is there one part of this recipe that's more important than the others. Is there something here that people get wrong??

The main thing is the air fuel ratio. That's what most people don't get right. They think the bigger the jet the more power they will get. But, if you add too much fuel the mixture is too rich and the fuel won't burn properly. The other mistake is, people don't understand the needle in the carb. Once you get the main jet right you can adjust the needle to bring the cruise range into that same 13.5 to one ratio. The main jet controls the high speed circuit. The needle controls the mid-range circuit. Mid-range is the circuit that you use for most riding. The pilot jet controls idle and just off-idle.

What about exhaust. Everyone changes the exhaust from stock. Is there one design that works better than another? Do two-into-one pipes work better than staggered duals (in general)? What about straight pipes?

With exhaust, the bigger the muffler the better it works but most riders don't like big mufflers. I prefer something with a baffle for overall power,

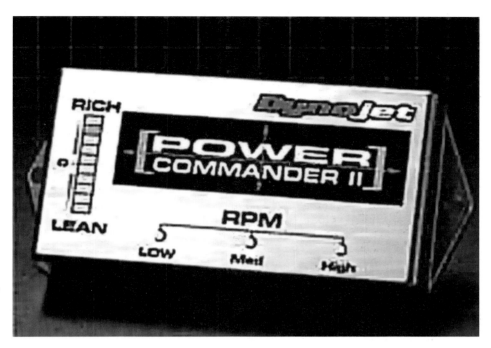

Fuel injected bikes run great, the question is, how to correct the air fuel ratio after making modifications to the engine. The answer is this Power Commander from Thunder Mfg.

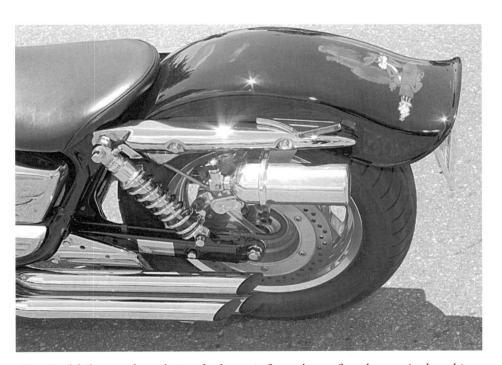

Hot Rod bikes need good visuals that reinforce the go-fast theme. And nothing says go-fast like a NOS bottle hanging off the bike.

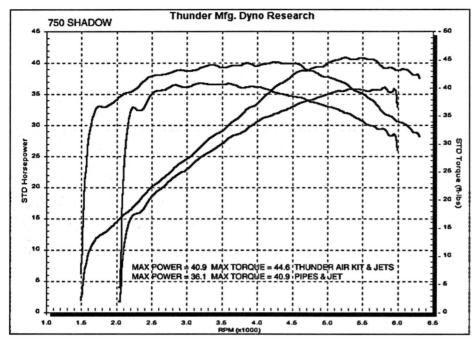

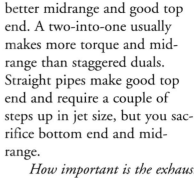

MAX POWER = 40.9 | MAX TORQUE = 44.6 | THUNDER AIR KIT & JETS
MAX POWER = 36.1 | MAX TORQUE = 40.9 | PIPES & JET

We live in the information age: Exactly how much power the bike will have after one or more modifications is only a mouse-click away. Thunder

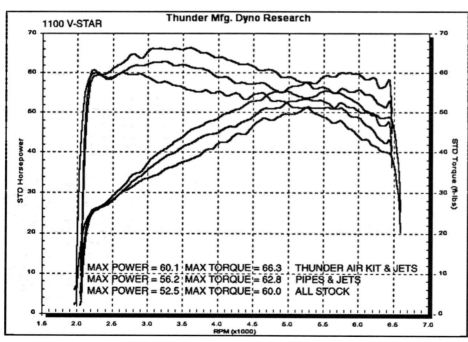

MAX POWER = 60.1 | MAX TORQUE = 66.3 | THUNDER AIR KIT & JETS
MAX POWER = 56.2 | MAX TORQUE = 62.8 | PIPES & JETS
MAX POWER = 52.5 | MAX TORQUE = 60.0 | ALL STOCK

This graph presents the stepped increases in horsepower and torque that come about through a series of modifications. The best results come from increases to both the intake and exhaust. Thunder

better midrange and good top end. A two-into-one usually makes more torque and midrange than staggered duals. Straight pipes make good top end and require a couple of steps up in jet size, but you sacrifice bottom end and midrange.

How important is the exhaust to the overall performance of the bike?

On a carbureted bike, on most of the bikes, the exhaust is important. With our dyno, with just a new exhaust on the bike we pick up four or five horsepower. Good exhaust helps to scavenge the cylinder. Typically, during the exhaust stroke not all the exhaust leaves, twenty percent of the old exhaust gas stays there. Better exhaust will clean out the cylinder better so maybe only ten percent of the old exhaust remains which means you get more fresh fuel and oxygen in the cylinder during the intake stroke and the engine makes more power.

You talked earlier about the need for the correct air fuel ratio. After the rider has installed exhaust or exhaust and a new air kit, how do they get the right jets?

This is an area where Thunder specializes. Most people install the parts and then take the bike to a tuner. When you buy a Thunder kit we tell you which jets and needles to install. I don't believe in seat of the pants testing. With our products, we show a graph that gives the before and after horsepower and torque readings.

What about getting the air fuel ratio right on the fuel injected Kawasakis.

There are a couple of different air kits available for the Kawasaki. We are currently the only ones who make a kit to change the air fuel ratio on the Kawasakis, that's our Power Commander. It goes in-line with the ECU unit, and adjusts the amount of fuel the injectors spray. The fuel injection on these bikes is precise and responds well to modifications. We pre-map the Power Commanders depending on what you've done to the bike, though there are buttons on the side of the unit that allow the customer to alter the low, mid and high range. We recommend they not do that however, because it's guess work.

With the fuel injected bike the pipes don't make as big a difference. We can take a new 1500, they are 54 horses stock. Then with the stock pipe and our air kit and a Power Commander we get them to 67 horsepower with the stock pipe. The horsepower only comes up to sixty eight or sixty nine with an aftermarket pipe.

How about results from a few of your kits on some other bikes?

The Road Star is a carbureted bike. They come in at fifty two horsepower stock. With pipes and our air kit the bike makes sixty four horsepower. We now have kits for 1100 V star and 650 Star too, both of those bikes come up eight or nine horsepower with our kits. We have dyno charts on our web site so people can see ahead of time how much additional power they are going to get. The results are pretty predictable, we've let *Cruiser* magazine have some of our kits. They install the kits and have the bikes run on a dyno and the results are at least as good as what we predict.

Variations on the staggered duals theme include these slash-cut classic pipes from Cobra.

If you like drag pipes, try this six-pipe set of drag pipes for the Valkyrie. Guaranteed to provide more power and a sound unlike anything you've ever heard. Cobra

Shop Time: Polishing

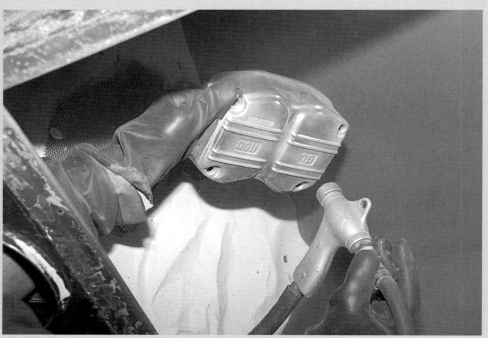

After stripping off the clearcoat, one of the first tasks is to bead blast the recesses in the cover.

In order to provide an inside look at what goes into a good polishing job we took an aluminum cam cover from a Goldwing to Deters Polishing in Spring Lake Park, Minnesota.

Joe Deters explained that the cover has a clear coat, often applied by the factory to keep aluminum parts from oxidizing and turning dark over time. "The first thing we have to do is to chemically strip off that clearcoat before we can start polishing," explained Joe. "Besides, the clearcoat is the first thing to fail on a part like this. That's what makes it so yellow and nasty looking."

The next step is a few minutes in the glass-bead cabinet where Joe uses a number ten bead to clean the paint and debris from the deep recesses on the cover. Sand blasting can't be used prior to polishing, because the sand leaves the surface too rough, and the sand becomes imbedded in the aluminum.

With the bead blasting finished the actual polishing can begin. Joe explains that the overall condition of the part determines how aggressive the first step should be. "Because this cover is in pretty good shape I'm using a 240 belt that's already broken in so it's not too aggressive." The work goes pretty fast and soon Joe is standing on the other side of the big polishing stand. The wheel Joe installs at this point is a

Because the cover is in pretty good shape, Joe starts with a fairly mild abrasive, a worn 240 grit belt.

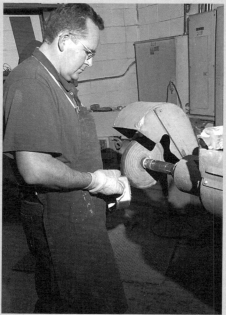

The flexible ribbed cotton wheel makes it easy to get down into the recesses in the cover.

Shop Time: Polishing

240 grit greaseless wheel used to clean up the recesses in the cover.

For polishing step number three Joe uses an Airflex wheel made of ribbed cotton. The abrasive that does the cutting at this stage is the Tripoli compound applied to the wheel as it spins. The idea of course is to work from a coarse to a very fine abrasive. "Each step along the way should remove the polishing marks left by the step before," is how Joe explains it.

"I change the angle occasionally," says Joe, "so I'm cutting ninety degrees to the previous cuts. This does a better job and also eliminates the likelihood I will leave a polishing pattern in the cover." When Joe is finished with the Tripoli compound on the cotton wheel the cover looks pretty good. In fact, at this point the cover is good enough to be chrome plated. But this cover came in for polishing, not chrome plating. This means there's still one step left. The color-buffing step.

Joe uses cut-and-color compound, also called simply a coloring compound. This very fine compound is applied to the same wheel as the one used in the step before. This final operation only takes about five minutes but the before-and-after difference is impressive. This final step really brings out the luster and the color of the aluminum.

It ain't cheap 'cause it ain't easy. Good polishing requires patience and a good understanding of the various steps.

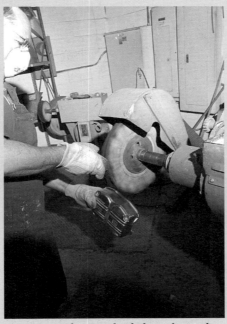

Compound is applied directly to the wheel, in such a way that "overspray" is directed onto the cover.

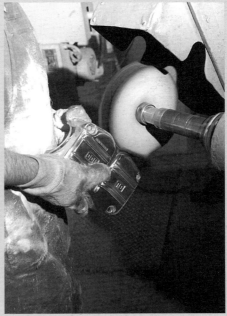

Joe dips his gloves in fresh flour for the final steps, to avoid staining the freshly polished cover.

Chapter Three

Suspension & Chassis

Shocks, Forks and Springs

When it comes to suspension systems and improvements to those systems there's a lot of ground to cover. We have to consider forks, which come in two flavors each of which can be further improved with the addition of chocolate syrup or crushed nuts. Then there are shocks to examine. Some bikes use two in a straightforward fashion, one on each side of the bike. Often, those two shocks are discarded in favor of only one mounted somewhere below the seat. Maybe we should start the discussion with an examination of the components that make up a good fork or shock absorber.

Orange Crush is he personal project of John Hoover from Kawasaki. The slammed profile is the result of shorter rear shocks, a Progressive lowering kit in the front fork and a set of 17 inch wheels and tires.

WHAT'S A SPRING?

A coil spring seems at first like the simplest thing in the world. Yet, there is more to a good spring, and choosing the right spring, than you might think. Coil springs are rated in weight/distance. For example, how many pounds of force does it take to compress the spring one inch? You could take the coil springs out of your fork and test their ratings with a ruler and a bathroom scale.

The simplest springs are linear in their strength. That is, if 200 pounds will compress the spring one inch, then 400 pounds will compress the same spring two inches (up to a certain limit of course). Some springs are said to be "progressive" meaning the coils are wound tighter on one end than the other, which essentially creates a spring with a variable rate. On soft bumps you compress only the more tightly wound coils. On harsh bumps those coils "coil bind" quickly leaving you with a spring that is essentially stiffer and better able to handle the larger bump.

NEED FOR A DAMPER

When you compress a spring and let go it doesn't just bounce back to its original position but rather goes well past that point and through a series of diminishing oscillations before coming back to the starting point. In order to dampen these up and down oscillations a shock absorber (technically these are dampers not shocks) is used, generally incorporated into the spring assembly.

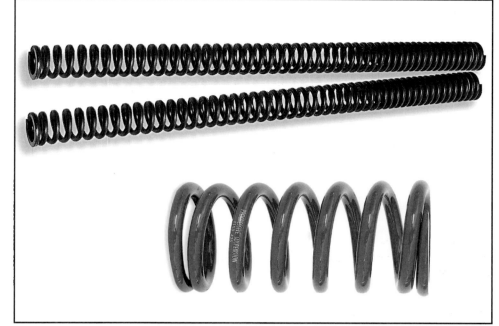

Springs come in every shape and size, from the progressive-wound fork springs to the larger spring meant for a single rear shock. Progressive

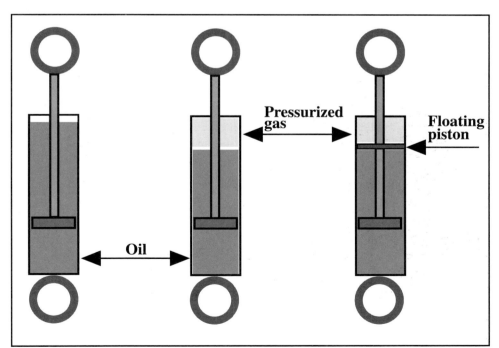

Gas-charged shocks aren't all the same inside. Some use a floating piston to separate the oil and gas. Some high quality shocks use no gas at all.

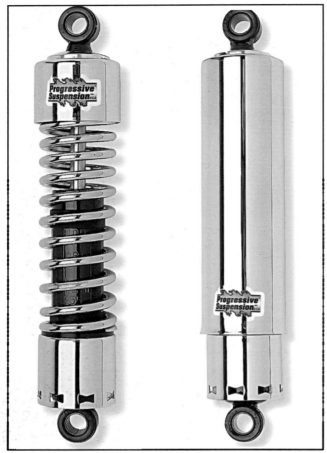

Popular with cruiser riders, the 412 shocks are offered in "conventional" styling as seen on the left, or with full chrome covers. Progressive

Shock Absorbers

The first shock absorbers were just "friction" shocks rubbing a series of rubber or leather discs together to dampen the up and down movement of the springs. Friction shocks exert the greatest resistance at the beginning of movement and then become easier to move once the "stiction" has been overcome. This is the exact opposite of the ideal characteristics found in a good damper unit. In place of friction between two discs, hydraulic dampers use the friction of a fluid moving through a restriction to dampen movement.

Looking at a modern shock it's easy to imagine the piston attached to the pushrod, moving through a cylinder filled with oil. The viscosity of the oil, it's quality and the size of the hole(s) that it passes through are the major factors affecting the stiffness of a particular shock absorber. Though the concept is simple, the actual innards of most mod-

ern shock absorbers are very sophisticated.

Most companies want different amounts of damping on compression and rebound. As Doug Cartney from Koni explained to me during work for an earlier tech article, "Koni has separate compression and rebound valves. The compression valve is called a 'foot valve,' it's a valve controlled by a stack of washers and is able to handle a very digressive velocity curve. When you hit a big bump you want the shock to be able to compress very rapidly. If you introduce too much damping on compression a bump can literally throw you off the bike."

"The rebound valve, on the other hand, is controlled by a coil spring. Like the compression valve, it's velocity sensitive but designed to offer a different damping curve. In the motorcycle shock absorber market, more money gets you more fea-

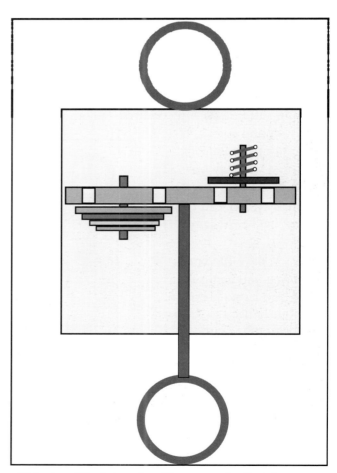

This simplified drawing illustrates the fact that compression and rebound valves are designed to control the movement of oil under very different conditions.

tures. Our top of the line shocks come with chrome bodies and adjustable rebound damping. The adjustment allows the user to change the size of an orifice, increasing or decreasing the effective size of the opening the oil passes through."

BUY QUALITY

Fluid friction provides the damping in a modern shock absorber. A shock that works hard on a bumpy road will heat up as the result of that friction. Inexpensive shocks allow air to mix with the oil, and the oil itself to change viscosity due to the heat. The net result is poor and inconsistent damping as the piston moves through an aerated froth of hot oil.

Inconsistent damping control and aerated oil are problems overcome by high quality shock absorbers. In a quality shock absorber, all the components, from pistons to shafts, are larger and built

Both the Valkyrie and the VTX 1800 come from the factory with a high quality upside down (inverted) fork.

For special needs or applications, Works will make up a pair of their one-off shocks designed specifically for your bike.

to higher standards. The valves that control the damping are much more sophisticated to better handle a variety of road conditions and riding styles. To better handle the heat, the amount of oil is increased. For better cooling, the body of the shock can be made of aluminum. To prevent aeration of the oil, the shock is gas-charged, or in some cases, filled with a premium oil that won't change viscosity.

When considering the benefits of replacing the original shocks with something from the aftermarket, it's good to consider the wise words of Blaine Birchfield from Cobra: "People have to remember that the OEM shocks (for most cruiser bikes) were all purchased on bid. The manufacturer told the supplier, 'I want a shock but it can't cost more than eleven dollars.' Almost anything you buy in the

Shop Time

Brad bought the shocks and springs as separate components so he could buy exactly the springs he wanted.

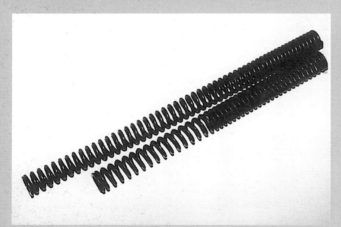

The new and old springs side by side - yes the old ones had sagged just a little.

The pinch bolts must be loosened to remove the caps on the top of the tubes.

AN EASY SUSPENSION UPGRADE

This sequence documents the suspension makeover on a 1990 VX 800 Suzuki. Brad Siqueiros, the bike's owner, felt the stock suspension was too soft and also wanted the bike to handle better.

The new front springs are from Progressive (their number 11-1129) and are in fact progressive in the way they are wound much tighter on one end than the other. These springs are designed to leave the bike at stock height, which is fine with Brad as lowering the bike was not one of his goals.

The rear shocks are likewise from Progressive, their "12" series. Though the shocks can be purchased complete, Brad bought the springs and shocks as separate pieces in order to buy heavier springs that would better accommodate his over 200 pound bulk. The springs are Progressive # 03-1368B, rated at 105/150 PSI.

FIX THE FORK

Brad's friend, Tom Heffrow, starts with the bike on the center stand. He puts a small screw jack under the front of the bike to hold up the front tire and fork. The Suzuki has no oil drain plug on the fork leg so Tom does not drain the fork oil.

The next step is to take off the nut on the top of each fork tube, after loosening the pinch bolt in the upper triple tree. The top nut comes off easily. In this case there is very little pre-load on the nut. Unlike some, it doesn't blast off like the cork in a bottle of champagne. The long collar comes out next. With a simple hook Tom reaches down and pulls out the spring itself. This rather simple disassembly is possible because Brad's bike did not need fork seals. Bikes that do need fork seals will require a complete disassembly of the front fork.

Next, Tom pulls the cap off the other fork

Shop Time

tube and pulls out the spring. To check the oil level against the chart that came with the springs Tom first compresses the fork all the way and locks it there with a 2x4 under the tire. A thin stick of wood makes a good "dip stick," ten weight oil is used to top-up the level in the tubes. "I prefer to drain the oil, that way you can measure exactly how much was in there and the oil gets changed too," explains Tom. "But in this case we just can't do it."

Reassembly is, as the manuals all say, "the reverse of disassembly." To elaborate slightly, Tom starts by dropping the new spring into the tube, followed by the required number of spacers, then the 2-1/2 inch pre-load spacers recommended by other Suzuki owners and then the top cap itself. Note: the information on the dimension of the pre-load spacers was found on the Suzuki owners web site (fuxharp.boston.ma.us/bikes/vx800faq). The 2-1/2 inch spacers were cut from schedule 80 PVC pipe, which is gray in color and tougher than the other grades.

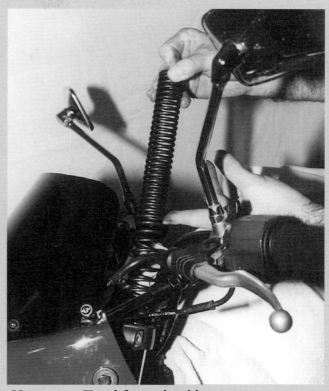

Here we see Tom lift out the old spring.

THE REAR SHOCKS

Installing the rear shocks is a pretty simple task. Tom starts the project by popping off the seat and removing the luggage rack. Next the tail-piece comes off, which in this case can be done without removing the muffler. Finally the first shock comes off.

It takes a little while to sort through the assortment of washers and spacers that come with the shocks. Tom puts a little grease on each shock stud,

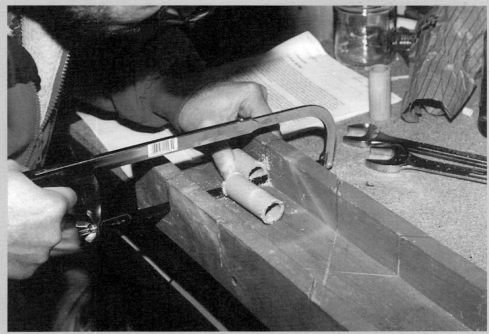

A simple miter box is a handy tool for cutting the pre-load spacers to length.

In The Shop

The seat, luggage rack and tail section must come off first in order to remove the two rear shocks.

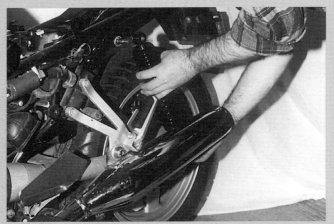

After assembling he shocks, Tom puts them on the bike one at a time.

between the stud and the metal tube or liner, and then slides the first shock into place with a soft mallet. To ensure the shock is seated on the studs Tom raps each end with a hammer and wooden drift. Then it's just a matter of tightening the nuts and starting in on the other side. The final task is the replacement of the tail section, luggage rack and seat.

Differences in the bike after the installation of the new springs and shocks become apparent as soon as Brad throws a leg over the Suzuki. With Brad on the seat the bike settles much less than it did originally. On the road the bike handles with more precision and no longer takes a deep "dive" each time Brad uses the front brake. The modest cost and relative ease with which the parts were installed leaves Brad wondering why he waited so long to improve the Suzuki's suspension.

The finished Suzuki. Though it might look the same, on the road it's a "whole new machine."

aftermarket is going to be much better than those original equipment shocks."

FORKS

Most forks used on street driven cruisers utilize what we call "right side up" designs. That is, the tubes, or smaller diameter part of the fork assembly, bolts to the triple clamp. The lower leg, the larger diameter part of the assembly with the caliper mounting lugs, slides up and down on the tubes. The spring that holds up the front of the bike is inside the tube, as is the fork oil.

A few cruisers; some Suzukis, the Valkyrie and the VTX 1800 use an "upside down" or inverted fork assembly. Used for some time on competition bikes, this design inverts the two major components that make up any fork. The larger diameter part of the fork, what we used to call the lower legs, is now bolted to the triple clamps. The tubes

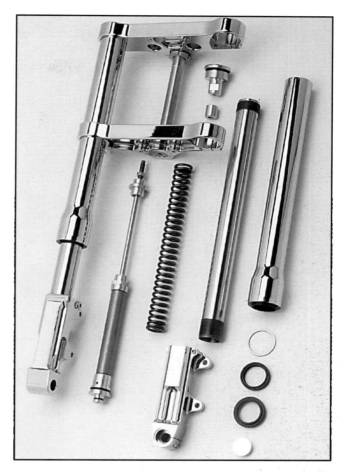

Exploded view of this Storz fork assembly shows the spring, seals and the cartridge. Storz

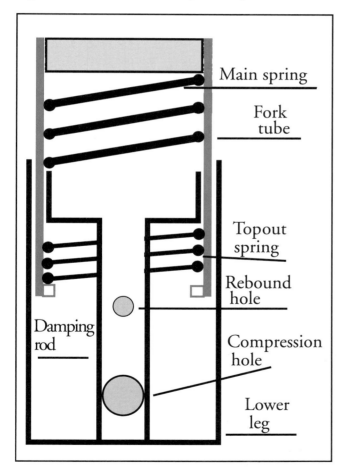

An oversimplified drawing showing the major parts in a typical damper-rod fork.

become the components that move up and down with the front wheel as it moves over bumps. By clamping the larger diameter member to the triple trees, with only enough of the smaller diameter "piston" protruding to mount the axle and allow for suspension travel, the inverted fork puts the strongest member in the triple trees - which reduces flex and makes for a more stable front end. This design also reduces unsprung weight by making the smaller diameter part of the fork the part that moves with the wheel over bumps.

Fork assemblies can be further divided according to how they dampen the action of the springs. Most conventional OEM designs use damper rods. More sophisticated fork assemblies are "cartridge style." These more sophisticated forks are more commonly seen on motocross and competition bikes.

These Gold Valve Cartridge Emulators make your damper rod fork assembly behave like a more sophisticated cartridge fork assembly. Race Tech

Damper-rod forks, as used on most new cruiser motorcycles, use oil moving through fixed holes in the damper rods to do the damping. The biggest problem with these forks is trying to make one "hole" fit all situations.

Cartridge forks use a tunable cartridge to control the damping. Similar to high quality shock absorbers, these sophisticated assemblies use a different valve for rebound and compression, each with its own damping curve. In this way the suspension engineer can design a fork with different damping action on rebound and compression. In addition, each one of these valves can open just a little for a small bump encountered at low speed, or a lot for a sharp-edged bump encountered at a higher speed. The spring loaded orifice changes size in response to your speed and the size of the bump you happen to encounter.

Some of the current offerings from the aftermarket allow you to modify a simple damper-rod fork to operate with the sophistication of a cartridge assembly. Race Tech offers a more sophisticated answer to your suspension woes - a Cartridge Fork Emulator. As Tom Hicks from Race Tech explained, "The problem with damping rod type forks is you're doing the damping by shoving oil through holes and those holes are always the same size. If you make them larger they work better on big bumps but worse on small bumps. If you make the

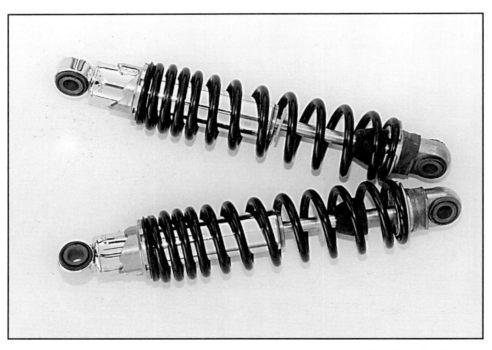

Koni makes a variety of shock absorber models, including these steel bodied shocks with adjustable cams and non-adjustable damping. Note the progressively wound springs.

holes too small, you get good control on slow-speed, small bumps but things get much worse on bigger, sharp edged bumps"

"Our Gold Valve Emulators drop in on top of the damper rods. To install them you drill the compression holes in the damper rods pretty big so they don't do any damping. Now, on compression, the oil goes to the emulator, which uses a spring loaded valve to do the damping. The emulator makes the fork work more like one of the new cartridge style forks."

LOWERING THE BIKE - HOW SHORT IS TOO SHORT

We all want our bikes "lowered." Before slamming the bike to the asphalt however, think about your overall plan for the bike and the effect of lowering on the way you ride. People who corner hard need more clearance between frame or floorboards and terra firma. What limits the cornering speed of most motorcycles is the clearance. You can only lean it over until things start to drag. And while you may consider yourself a slow rider, there might be that one afternoon when you come into a corner too fast and need all the clearance you can find to get around the bend.

Lowering the front

The easiest way to lower the front of the bike is with a lowering kit like that sold by Progressive Suspension, Race Tech, or

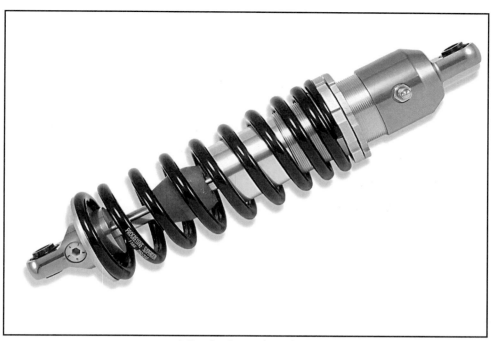

This high quality 420 series shock, available for the Road Star, comes in standard length and one inch shorter to lower the back of the bike. Progressive

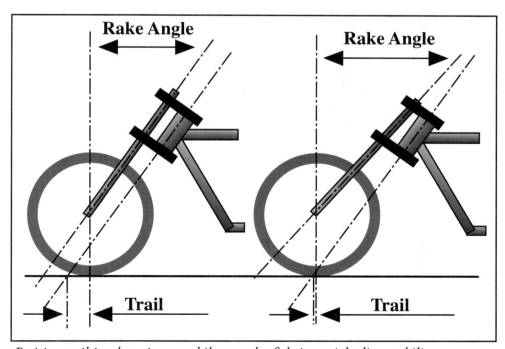

Positive trail is what gives our bikes much of their straight-line stability. Normally, extra rake means extra trail as well. Raked triple trees, however, can eliminate most or all of that trail.

47

New billet triple trees can be used to improve the looks of the front end, and/or create the wide-glide effect by moving the fork tubes farther apart. Planet Cruiser

one of the other companies in the Cruiser market. The kit from Progressive Suspension includes new fork springs, new top-out springs and new pre-load spacers. The kit can be used to lower the bike either one or two inches. The kit from Race Tech offers the same one or two inch option, and comes with or without their cartridge fork emulators as well as the new springs. All this assumes you are working with a mostly stock bike with standard diameter wheels.

Though some might consider it cheating, many fork and triple tree combinations allow you to loosen the pinch bolts that hold the tubes in the trees, and then slide the fork tube up in the triple trees (be sure the bike is on a jack before you try this). Done in moderation you can often lower the front of the bike an inch or more in this way. Bikes with fairings are likely candidates as the fairing will hide the top of the fork leg sticking out of the top triple tree.

Lowering the back of the bike

The ease with which the rear of your bike can be lowered depends on the type of suspension. The standard twin-shock rear suspension simply requires shorter shocks. How much shorter? Well, most will want the back of the bike level with the front. Before ordering one inch shorter shocks to lower the bike one inch in back, remember that for most bikes it's not a one-to-one ratio. If you want the rear lowered one inch, call the shock manufacturer and ask them which length of shock manufactured for your bike will give the desired results. And as mentioned farther along, you can't just order shocks by length.

The evolving metric aftermarket offers a variety of solutions for anyone who wants to lower the rear of a single-shock bike. Progressive Suspension offers their very high quality rear

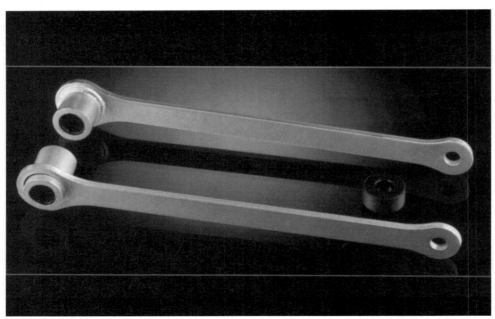

This lowering kit is designed for the rear of your favorite Road Star. Planet Cruiser.

shock for the Road Star in two lengths: standard and one inch shorter. Baron Custom Accessories makes kits for the all the Yamaha Star bikes. Road Star owners can buy a rear shock relay arm made of 7075 billet aluminum that will lower the rear a full inch and a half. The kit does require bearings, seals and collars that must be purchased from the dealer. V-Star 1100 owners can buy new rear suspension links that achieve the same degree of lowering men-

"Lowering" the bike includes things like paint jobs with horizontal stripes and seats that blend into the rear fender.

tioned above. Even the 650 V-Star owners are covered here, with a lowering bracket that replaces the stock shock's upper mounting eyelet to achieve the same inch and a half subtraction to ground clearance. Planet Cruiser is another company with a variety of lowering kits for many of the single-shock bikes.

There is one more type of lowering that should be mentioned before we leave this chapter. Instead of lowering the bike physically, you can lower it visually. For more on this check out the ideas in the Chapter Seven, Styling.

SAFETY WARNINGS AND DISCLAIMERS

Remember that lowering the bike makes the suspension's job that much more difficult. A typical stock shock absorber might have five inches of travel. Five inches to absorb the energy of a big bump. When you cut that travel nearly in half the shock's job is nearly twice as hard. It's left with only three inches of travel during which it must absorb the same amount of energy. So understand that there are trade-offs. A decrease in travel means the ride will be more harsh. It's a matter of physics.

The other caution involves the choice of the new shorter shocks (or any new shocks for that matter). The shock manufacturer must figure more

A quick and easy way to drop the front end - just slide the tubes up slightly in the triple trees.

than just the extended and compressed dimensions of the shock absorber. The weight of the bike, the length of the swingarm and position of the shock absorber on the swingarm are all important considerations as well. What this means is that you can't just buy a shock that looks like yours but is one or two inches shorter. You need to buy a shock designed for your particular motorcycle that will give the correct ride height.

There is nothing much

This clean and sanitary Road Star is a project bike from Barron Custom Accessories featuring many of their parts, including the lowering kits.

cooler than a slammed bike. Like everything else however, the slamming has a cost. First, there's the hit to the wallet. Then the busted knuckles (or another hit to the wallet). Finally, there's the trade off in ground clearance and overall ride. Be sure you understand all the costs before taking the low road.

INTERVIEW WITH LARRY LANGLEY AT PROGRESSIVE SUSPENSION

Larry, can we start by talking about the Kawasaki project bike, Orange Krush. John Hoover at Kawasaki says you were instrumental in lowering the bike. Can you tell us what you did to the front and rear suspension.

We used eleven inch rear shocks, and then used one of our kits to lower the front forks two inches. Two inches is the maximum we like to see a street bike lowered.

I tell people who want to lower their bike to stick with lowering it one inch. That way it looks good and you still have enough travel that the suspension can work the way it should.

What do people give up by lowering the bike too far?

You have a shock that had four inches of travel

This block is the lowering "kit" sold by Barron to drop the back of your Road Star.

These premium 418 shocks from progressive are built with aluminum bodies and allow user adjustment of rebound damping. Progressive

bike. What length you need depends on the bike, and how far you want to lower it. You can't just take the shorter shocks from your buddy's Yamaha and use them on your Kawasaki.

What kind of mistakes do people make when they lower their bikes?

They use the brackets that move the lower shock mounting point instead of the correct shorter shock. When we sell you a shorter shock, it's designed to have the same compressed length as the stock length shock and how it has two. It has half the distance to do the same amount of work. In order to make sure the bike won't bottom on a bump the springs have to be much stiffer, and the damping has to be firmer as well. The more you lower the bike the more ride quality you give up. Travel equals comfort.

Can you talk about what goes into one of your front end lowering kits and how much do they drop the front of the bike.

Our kits let you lower the fork one or two inches. You get a pair of springs, they're really spacers, and a new main spring. You can install either one or two of these "spacers" to lower it one or two inches. Essentially, when you reassemble the fork it's compressed part way. You've given up travel again.

On bikes with twin shocks in the rear, like the Kawasaki project bike, can people just order shorter shocks by specifying the length they want?

No, because each bike is different, depending on the lever ratio: shock travel vs. rear wheel travel. If the shock moves one inch, for example, now far does the rear wheel move? It's not always the same. So you have to order the shock for a particular

As this Honda demonstrates, the vast bulk of current cruisers continue to use the conventional or right-side-up front fork.

51

This close up shows the single shock rear suspension used on the Victory motorcycle. The Victory dealer with a bike in the Dream Bikes section lowered his by modifying the shock. Works Performance could probably make or modify a shock for your Victory.

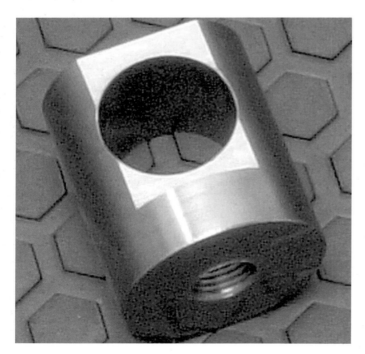

Barron understands that owners of the smaller bikes may want to lower their bikes too, so they designed this lowering "kit" for Yamaha V-Star 650s.

did, so the tire won't hit the fender for example. With the brackets I mentioned, you've lowered the bike and changed the point where the wheel travel stops. Now the wheel will travel closer to the fender before the movement stops. We don't recommend the brackets at all.

The other mistake people make is they lower them too far so there's no real suspension left.

Can you describe what goes into a quality shock absorber and what you get as you spend more money on the shock(s)?

Quality shocks are built with damping and springs that match and will last a reasonable length of time. Our shocks are engineered for 50,000 to 100,00 miles. We have documented usage of well over 200,000 miles. The more money you spend the more sophisticated the shock is with more features. For example, our 412 series shock retails for about $250 a pair. 412s are steel bodied, gas charged, preload adjustable with non-adjustable damping. A very good shock for the money.

The next step up is our 418 series, these have an aluminum body, adjustable rebound and they're rebuildable. The custom bike guys really like this shock and it retails for about $450 per pair. The top of the line 440 series features stare of the art Inertia Active System (IAS) damping that can soak up any road imperfection like you can't believe. They retail for about $495 a pair. You can get a more in-depth look at our suspension systems and how they work by checking out our web site at progressivesuspension.com.

Unsprung Weight and Shocks

At this point we need to digress and discuss sprung and unsprung weight, terms you're likely to see if you pick up a book or article about suspension design for cars or bikes. It's also a factor you should consider when trying to decide which shocks, brakes and wheels to buy. Most of the motorcycle, that is the frame, engine sheet metal and all the rest are considered sprung weight: weight supported by the springs. The wheels and tires, lower fork and brake components on the other hand are considered unsprung weight.

Consider a motorcycle running down the road, it hits a sharp bump in the pavement which forces the wheel up while compressing the spring. One of the goals of any good suspension system is to keep the tires on the pavement. When the bump in question drops away quickly you want the wheel to change direction rapidly and stay in contact with the asphalt.

The problem (one of the problems anyway) is the momentum of the wheel and tire, which makes them want to continue in an upward direction even after the pavement is falling away. The compressed spring is trying to force apart the wheel and the frame. How much of the spring's energy raises the bike and how much of it forces the tire down to maintain its grip with the road depends on the ratio of sprung to unsprung weight.

A lighter wheel/tire/brake assembly will react more quickly to irregularities in the road while feeding less energy into the rest of the motorcycle.

You also have to consider the shock absorber's role in this scenario. To quote Doug from Koni: "Compression damping controls unsprung weight, how fast the wheel and brake assembly moves up toward the rest of the bike. Rebound damping controls the sprung weight, the bike and rider. We only let you change the rebound damping, because the sprung weight is what you typically change between rides. You add a passenger or you add gear which changes the amount of sprung weight."

Unsprung weight

The bike can be divided into two parts, sprung and unsprung weight. The wheels, tires, calipers/rotors and a percentage of the fork or swingarm are considered unsprung weight. By keeping these components light you make the suspension's job that much easier.

Chapter Four

Wheels and Tires

Defining the Motorcycle

They hold up the motorcycle; contribute greatly to the bike's ride, handling and turn-in; have a major impact on the machine's unsprung weight; and profoundly affect how the bike sits and looks. Yes, the wheels and tires are a very important part of your project.

WHEELS

The wheels constitute two of the biggest visual elements on the motorcycle. Because of their size they help to "define" the motorcycle. Given their

A big believer in the use of billet wheels, Jeff Palhegyi installed spoked billet wheels from RC Components on Wild Child.

importance the hard part is deciding which, if any, wheels to add to the machine during the makeover.

Wheels break down into two broad categories: billet and spoked. Up until recently there weren't a large number of billet wheels available for the shaft-drive cruisers, due to the expense of manufacturing different rear wheels, each with the correct hub. This situation is now changing for two reasons: The expanding cruiser market demands billet wheels for cruisers, and most of the manufacturers have designed their wheels as modular assemblies. The hub, designed for a particular brand of bike, bolts to a "universal" wheel. This means one wheel can fit a large number of bikes from different manufacturers.

Having said all that, there are still more wheels available for a belt-drive bike like a Yamaha Road Star than for a Honda A.C.E. Some of the catalogs only list wheels for the front wheel for this reason. With a belt drive bike like a Victory you may even be able to adapt a wheel meant for the Harley market to your cruiser. Many of the wheels designed for belt-drive bikes are part of a complete line of matching parts that includes brake rotors and the rear belt pulley.

BILLET AND CAST WHEELS

Most are referred to by

Even on a "bagger" the wheels are a very big part of what people see when they look at a bike.

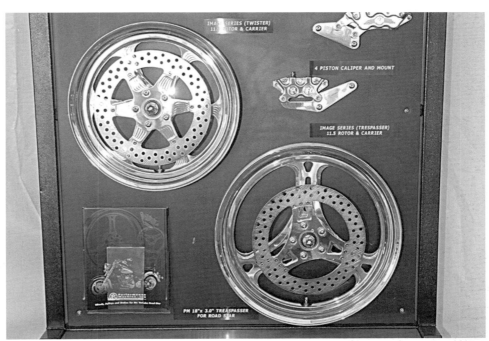

The big manufacturers displays often have a variety of wheels mounted to the peg board so you can get a better idea what's available.

Another Jeff Palhegyi bike with another set of RC wheels. RC and PM both make pulleys and rotors that match their wheels.

the name "billet" but that doesn't mean that aluminum wheels are all the same in terms of strength, weight and price. What we call billet wheels come in a variety of designs made from more than one alloy and type of aluminum.

What might be called true billet wheels are carved from a billet (or a solid chunk) of aluminum. In most cases the aluminum in question is 6061 T6, the first four digits identify this as forged aluminum of a certain alloy while the T6 number refers to the heat treating specification.

Billet aluminum wheels are expensive for at least two reasons. First, the chunks of raw, forged aluminum don't come cheap. Second, there's considerable machine time in each wheel, creating the spokes and shapes that define the many models from all the manufacturers.

The cost of an aluminum wheel can be reduced by casting the wheel, generally from an alloy identified as 356 aluminum. This eliminates the expense of buying forged billets of aluminum, though tooling costs for cast wheels can be high. By casting the spokes as part of the wheel design these wheels need less time on the milling machines which further reduces their cost. Most cast wheels have a rim that is an integral part of the assembly. One potential problem with cast wheels is the porosity of the cast material which makes it more diffi-

This Tresspasser from Performance machine is available for the Road Star in 16 and 18 inch sizes for both front and rear. Compatible with stock or PM rotors and pulleys. PM

cult to chrome plate a cast wheel.

In the past there were some true billet wheels that utilized spokes (or a center section) cut from forged aluminum, bolted or welded to a separate rim assembly. Currently most billet wheels are made by carving the wheel and rim (the hub may be a separate bolt-on piece) from one piece of forged billet aluminum. The process is called split and spin, and uses specialized tooling to form the rim as an integral part of the billet wheel. (See the interview with Pierre Elliott in this chapter for more on billet wheels.)

When deciding which wheels to buy consider the fact that it's hard to beat the strength-to-weight ratio of 6061 aluminum. In most cases a true billet wheel is lighter and stronger than a very similar appearing cast wheel. Cast wheels, because of differences in the two alloys, may not be able to match the polished finish seen on a billet wheel. Because 6061 is stronger, billet wheels may offer designs and details that can't be matched in a cast wheel.

When you buy those new aluminum wheels be sure you get what you pay for. If you're paying billet prices be sure the wheels are billet aluminum.

WHEEL SIZES

Currently, most of the manufacturers of billet wheels offer front wheels in four or five different diameters, including 16, 17, 18, 19 and 21 inches. Widths include a skinny 2.15 inches for the 21-inch hoops, to a more typical 3 or 3.5 inches for a 16 or 17 inch wheel.

Rear wheels come in 16, 17, and 18 inch diameters. Widths start at an OEM-like 3 inches and stretch all the way to 5 and 5.5 inches. Like other two and four-wheeled enthusiasts, cruiser

A project bike from Performance Machine that illustrates the benefits of using billet wheels with matching rotors and rear pulley.

Inspired by the old American racing mag, this twelve-spoke design from PM is available in 16 and 18 inch diameters. Rear wheels come in widths up to 5.5 inches.

There's nothing wrong with spokes wheels, they lend a nice classic look to any bike they're mounted on.

riders are looking for wider rubber on the rear wheel. Many of the bikes out there will take a wider tire than the one planted under the fender by the manufacturer. John Hoover from Kawasaki squeezed a 180 series Dunlop tire on his Vulcan classic, mounted on 17 by 5.5 inch rim from RC Components, though John reports the installation did involve "removal of just a little metal on the driveshaft housing."

SPOKED WHEELS - SPOKES, HUBS AND RIMS

Spoked wheels lend a certain classic elegance to nearly any motorcycle and many of the current cruisers come to market with nothing fancier than a pair of laced wheels.

Given the price of billet it makes a certain amount of sense to retain the spoked wheels that came with your cruiser. With a bit of ingenuity you can add a wider rim to the existing hub and connect the two with twisted or diamond-cut stainless spokes.

The trouble with this scenario is the fact that the spoke pattern on the hub must match the pattern on the rim. And rims drilled for metric hubs are in very short supply. Harley rims generally use 40 spokes, while most metric cruisers use 48 or more. There are some interesting options here, however. In order to better understand those options we called Kenny Buchanan from Buchanan's Spoke and Rim.

As Kenny explained, "a lot of people are realizing these are pretty good bikes and they aren't all over the place, they're not very common. Those people are looking at the wheels, wondering what can they do. To start with you have to work with a cruiser that already has wire wheels, there are no custom hubs available."

Kenny explains that what you can do is lace a custom rim up to an existing metric hub with your choice of stainless spokes. "We just did two wheels for a Yamaha Road Star," explains Kenny. "The stock wheels are 16 inches front and rear. This guy is doing a full custom bike so we laced up a 4.25X18 inch wheel for the rear and a 2.75X19 inch rim for the front."

The rims Kenny laced onto the Yamaha hub are extruded aluminum rims from Sun. They come undrilled, meaning a company like Buchanan's can drill them for any spoke pattern. Diameters include 16, 17, 18, 19 and 21 inches with rim widths that start at 1.60 inches on the 21 inch rim and go to 4.25 inch on the 16, 17 and 18 inch rims. The 4.25 inch rim means the widest tire you can "legally" run is a 150 series tire. (see the Tire section that follows for more on which tire will fit which rim.)

This well-known Cobra bobber couldn't be built with anything but spoked wheels.

Though all spoked wheels look alike at first glance, this Yamaha assembly with chrome plated rim uses a different number of spokes that does a wheel designed for the typical American V-Twin.

"We also have spun aluminum rims as wide as 5.5X18 inches," explains Kenny, "that we can drill for the various metric hubs." Kenny says the Sun rims are stronger, "they were originally built for motocross use" but that there's really nothing wrong with the spun aluminum rims.

Even if you don't go to the trouble of lacing in a wider rim, you might want to consider new stainless spokes. Kenny describes the stock spokes as "cadmium plated or maybe flash-chromed. Which means they only really look good for about a year. We have stainless spokes in a variety of styles including twisted and diamond cut."

Whether you simply add stainless spokes, or lace in a wider rim so you can add a wider tire, the wheels should be assembled and trued by an experienced person, as they're often harder to true than a typical Harley-Davidson wheel.

HOW MUCH DO THEY WEIGH?

The weight of the numerous wheel assemblies varies enormously. Why should you care? Because of that old issue of unsprung weight (discussed in Chapter Three). A lighter wheel/tire/brake assembly will react more quickly to irregularities in the road while feeding less energy into the rest of the motorcycle. A light wheel has the added advantage of being quicker to accelerate when you drop the hammer, which is another reason why drag and road race bikes run the lightest wheels available.

TIRES - WHAT ALL THOSE NUMBER MEAN

Motorcycle tires, at least the good ones, come with a enough type on the sidewall to make up a short

These spoked rims, manufactured in Europe, are available for a number of the current cruisers. Planet Cruiser

novel. The story here is non-fiction however, and very important. All the tire manufacturers publish technical and fitment data for their full range of tires. Taking a page from the Avon data book, one of the two tires recommended for the rear of a Kawasaki Vulcan Classic is a 150/80-16 71V TL AM 18 Supervenom.

Understanding the code: The first numbers give the approximate section width of the tire in millimeters. This is the width of the tire through a section just outside the rim and not the width of the tire at its widest point. The second number describes the profile. The number 80 means the tire is 80 percent as tall as it is wide. A 40 would represent a very low-profile tire, one that is only 40 percent as tall as it is wide. The next number, sixteen, represents the applicable tire diameter while the 71 is the load index, a numerical code associated with the maximum load a tire can carry at the speed indicated by the speed symbol. In the example above, V is the speed symbol, the maximum speed at which the tire can carry a load corresponding to its load index. The TL means the tire is tubeless and must be mounted on a tubeless-type rim. The AM18 is the model specific identification code. The Avon book identifies this as a rear-tire designed to "Maintain a wide contact patch and even weight distribution for better

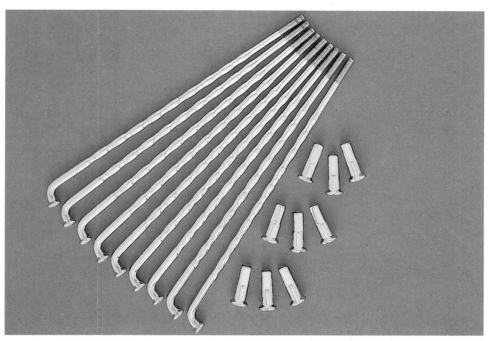

If you have your rim relaced, or add a wider rim to the current hub, consider using something like these twisted stainless spokes. Nempco

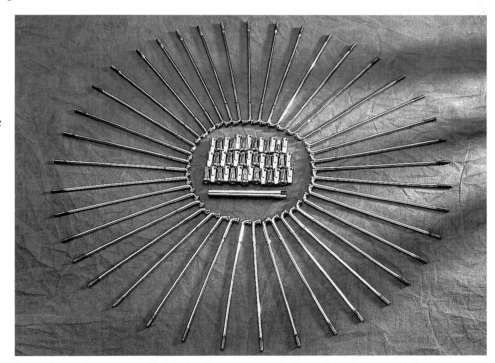

Straight spokes are available in chrome or stainless, though most of the pros seem to prefer the stainless. Drag Specialties

handling and ride at higher lean angles for the aggressive rider."

Tires sold in the US market also carry a load rating designated as B or C. To quote Craig Knapp from Hoppe and Associates, the US Avon distributor, "A C-range is most often a tire reinforced with additional belting or plies, usually Kevlar, Rayon or Nylon. The B or C rating will be marked on the sidewall of the tire but rarely advertised. Most list maximum inflated pressure for the Cs at 50psi while the Bs usually top out at about 42psi."

THE SPEED RATINGS

All tires carry a speed rating. These ratings start at S, good up to 112 miles per hour; H, good up to 130 miles per hour; V, 150 miles per hour and W good up to 169 miles per hour. Looking through the Avon chart again, tires rated VB and VR can be run at speeds up to 210 kilometers per hour (roughly 131 miles per hour), the ZR can operate at speeds up to 150 miles per hour while the V300 is good to 186 miles per hour. The chart does contain the caveat that the VB, VR and ZR tires can be operated at the maximum speed "at reduced loading." Apparently the tire manufacturers don't want you attempting top speed runs on your ZX-12 while the bike is loaded down with camping gear or ridden two up.

Tire data sheets and catalogs from the major manufacturers contain some kind of warning that "replacement tires should be exact replacements for the originals and bear the same speed and load index as those fitted when the bike was new." Of course, most of us never take the time to read the fine print at the bottom of the page. All we want is the best, the widest, tire we can get on the back

Size	Service Description (Load Index / Speed Symbol)		Rec Rim	Rim Width Range (ins)		Section Width		Overall Width		Overall Diameter		Static Loaded Radius		Revs. per		Maximum Pressure		Maximum Load		Maximum Speed	
				Min.	Max.	mm	ins	mm	ins	mm	ins	mm	ins	km	mile	bar	psi	kg	lbs	km/h	mph
SUPER VENOM AM20 FRONT																					
100/90 V 16	54	V	MT2.50	2.15	2.75	103	4.1	109	4.3	585	23.0	281	11.1	567	913	2.9	42	212	467	210	130
																		180	397	240	149
100/90 V 18	56	V	MT2.50	2.15	2.75	99	3.9	107	4.2	636	25.0	307	12.1	519	835	2.9	42	224	494	210	130
																		190	419	240	149
110/90 V 16	59	V	MT2.50	2.15	3.00	113	4.4	120	4.7	603	23.7	289	11.4	551	887	2.9	42	243	536	210	130
																		207	456	240	149
110/90 V 18	61	V	MT2.50	2.15	3.00	111	4.4	114	4.5	655	25.8	314	12.4	506	814	2.9	42	257	567	210	130
																		218	482	240	149
120/80 V 16	60	V	MT2.75	2.50	3.00	116	4.6	123	4.8	603	23.7	288	11.3	552	888	2.9	42	250	551	210	130
																		213	468	240	149
SUPER VENOM AM18 REAR																					
100/90 V 19 ◆	57	V	MT2.50	2.15	2.75	102	4.0	108	4.3	669	26.3	323	12.7	494	795	2.9	42	230	507	210	130
																		196	431	240	149
110/90 V 18 ◆	61	V	MT2.50	2.15	3.00	111	4.4	116	4.6	657	25.9	315	12.4	505	813	2.9	42	257	567	210	130
																		218	482	240	149
120/80 V 16 ◆	60	V	MT2.75	2.50	3.00	115	4.5	120	4.7	603	23.7	290	11.4	550	885	2.9	42	250	551	210	130
																		213	468	240	149
120/80 V 18 ◆	62	V	MT2.75	2.50	3.00	117	4.6	121	4.8	658	25.9	316	12.4	505	813	2.9	42	265	584	210	130
																		225	496	240	149
120/90 V 18	65	V	MT2.75	2.50	3.00	118	4.6	121	4.8	670	26.4	323	12.7	493	793	2.9	42	290	639	210	130
																		247	543	240	149
130/80 V 18	66	V	MT3.00	2.50	3.50	124	4.9	132	5.2	667	26.3	323	12.7	495	797	2.9	42	300	661	210	130
																		255	562	240	149
130/90 V 17	68	V	MT3.00	2.50	3.50	129	5.1	131	5.2	661	26.0	316	12.4	504	811	2.9	42	315	694	210	130
																		268	590	240	149
140/70 V 18	67	V	MT4.00	3.50	4.50	145	5.7	155	6.1	653	25.7	312	12.3	510	821	2.9	42	307	677	210	130
																		261	575	240	149
150/80 V 16	71	V	MT3.50	3.00	4.25	152	6.0	158	6.2	646	25.4	310	12.2	513	826	2.9	42	345	761	210	130
																		293	646	240	149
MT90 -16	74	V	3.00D	2.50	3.50	127	5.0	131	5.2	634	25.0	303	11.9	527	858	2.9	42	375	827	210	130
																		319	703	240	149

A partial page from the Avon tire-data book - material that's well worth reviewing before buying new tires for that cruiser.

Current billet wheel designs include the somewhat organic design seen on top, and the ultra modern razor design seen on the bottom. PM

with a lower profile and a lower load index number, than that recommended by the bike's manufacturer. The tire may fail because low-profile tires have a smaller volume of air inside, which diminishes their ability to handle the heat that results from heavy loads carried at highway speeds.

The information published by the manufacturers for each tire includes the ideal rim width. If you mount a given tire on a rim of the bike. Finding that "best" tire for your cruiser is easier if you have the data book from the tire manufacturer, the one with all the relevant facts and figures.

WHAT TO BUY

When buying tires, it's a good idea to buy them in sets. To quote Craig from Avon, "different brands and models of tires have specific shapes or contours (as in looking at a tire head-on) and not all are perfectly compatible. We as manufacturers don't test our fronts with some else's rears or vise-versa. A half-worn tire no longer has the same contour as the new one, and wear patterns can differ from bike-to-bike. If you're mixing tires of different mileage or brand, don't expect optimum performance."

This advice to stick close to OE recommendations definitely applies to radials. Some bikes are not considered suitable for radials. It's better to stick with the type of tire the bike came with. Definitely avoid any temptation to mix one radial with one non-radial tire.

Anyone who tours or loads the bike heavily needs to note the load ratings of any tires they mount. In particular it's dangerous to mount a tire

These wire wheels with polished alloy rims come in a variety to sizes for a number or cruisers. Planet Cruiser

63

The side wall provide a wealth of information, including the load range and speed rating, as well as the country of origin.

PM wheels will work with either the stock rotors and pulleys or their own matching rotors and pulleys as seen here. PM

wider than that recommended, the tire does get wider, though you can only go so far. The 200/60X16 Avon tire is 7.9 inches wide when mounted on the recommended 5.5 inch rim. The widest rim Avon recommends using with that tire is 6.25 inches wide, which will result in the same tire having a width of about 8.5 inches.

HOW FAT IS FAT

Everyone wants a fat tire on the back of their bike. Though the recommended tire for the Kawasaki recommended above is a 150/80, plenty of riders are installing a 170 and even a few 180-series tires on the back. The best recommendation as to what will fit can be had by asking other riders what they installed and how much trouble it was to install. As long as we're talking about tires we need to mention the fact that a 180/60-16 from Avon might not be exactly the same width as a tire of the same "dimension" from Metzeler or Dunlop. When following someone else's recommendation for a fat tire, note the tire brand and also the width of the rim they chose.

Craig from Avon suggests turning the normal wheel/tire buying sequence on its head. Instead of buying wheels first and then shopping for tires to mount, "pick out the tires first. Many buyers purchase custom wheels only

mine how much you've altered the final gear ratio.

In most situations you need to choose a tire with a diameter close to that of the original equipment tires, and a width that won't interfere with the swingarm, driveshaft or belt.

Remember that a wider tire may rub, not just on the obvious things like the driveshaft tube, but the inside of the fender where the little wiring-harness tabs stick out.

"Bug" from Kokesh shows us the only way to install a new tube-style tire - with a new tube inside the tire.

to find that the 'fat' tire they've been drooling over isn't a available in that wheel size. The most common problem is in 17 inch sizes. Avon, like most other tire builders, sees the 17 inch market as dominated by softer-compound Z-rated radials for sportbikes. With very few 17 inch original applications on cruisers, tire selection in this size is extremely limited. This all goes back to the very important issue of load and speed ratings as well as the original fitment argument. These 17 inch Z-speed rated tires have considerably less tread depth than the conventional bias H and V rated OE tires on most cruisers, have lower load ratings and get rather dismal mileage on heavy, torque laden twins. Without a doubt the wheels with the largest selection of possible tires are the 16 and 18 inch diameters."

Changing the diameter of the rear tire, either by changing the diameter of the rim or by changing the profile of the tire, will effectively change both the ground clearance and the gearing. Along with all those other numbers on the data charts for each tire is the total diameter, and the number of revolutions the tire makes per kilometer and per mile. This information can be used to deter-

You might think your 150 is a pretty beefy tire, until some one pulls up next to you with a 200 series tire.

Before running out to buy the trickest Metzeler or Avon tire that money can buy, remember that a lower profile tire changes more than just the amount of clearance between the frame and the ground. You also have to understand that a low profile tire gives the bike a much different look while also affecting the handling.

To turn a bike at speed you need to first lean it over. At that point the front tire can be compared to a Styrofoam coffee cup – one that always rolls toward the small end. The shape of the coffee cup determines the path it takes as it rolls over the surface of the table. The shape of the front tire is critical to the way the bike turns. Which is why many motorcycle tires are designed for the front or back and should never be swapped. Some are dual fitment but must still be mounted so they rotate in a specific direction. If in doubt, ask questions from the shop where you buy the tires.

Before leaving the topic of tires, we need to issue a few warnings to anyone new to this business of buying and possibly mounting motorcycle tires.

THINGS YOUR MOTHER WARNED YOU ABOUT (OR SHOULD HAVE)

First, always use a new tube with a new tire. There is abrasion between the tire and tube as the tire rotates. Even if the tube you pull out of the tire looks great, replace it with a new one. Likewise, anytime you get a flat, just buy a new tube. You may have to patch a tube to get home, but once there take it all apart again and install the new tube. Finally, if you aren't familiar with installing tires, you might want to let the local shop install the new tires. At least buy two good tire irons and maybe a protective rim cover to avoid putting big gouges in that new billet aluminum rim. Always spend the extra money to have the new tire and wheel assembly balanced.

A few tires in the catalogs carry no speed rating and no brand name either. Considering that it's your sorry butt riding on that seat it doesn't make any sense to buy anything less than the very best tires for that cool customized cruiser.

In terms of safely, comfort and appearance, the tires and wheels are probably the most important parts on the motorcycle. They must be chosen with care. When you upgrade to a better or a wider tire, be certain to give careful consideration to your choices. The tires must fit in a physical sense. They must also be a good "fit" for your particular machine in terms of the speed and load ratings.

INTERVIEW WITH PIERRE ELLIOTT, owner of Diamond Distributing, manufacturer of billet wheels.

Pierre, let's get some background on you, how did you get involved in the manufacture of wheels.

Originally I was very involved in drag racing and

These Road Star Pulleys are designed to match the various wheel designs. PM

it kind of evolved from there. I worked for a Kawasaki and Suzuki store in Connecticut and later for another Suzuki store and then a high performance store before my wife and I moved to Florida.

After we moved I started Diamond Racing Incorporated which is now Diamond Distributing. In addition to wheels we sell a variety of lubrication and high performance products at both the retail and wholesale level.

Wheels from Diamond Distributing are machined from a one piece blank for great strength. Hubs are separate bolt-on assemblies

The other thing every new tire needs is a good balance job before it goes on the bike.

Manufacturing wheels came about partly because of a conversation I had with John Hoover from Kawasaki in June of 1998. At the time I was selling a tremendous number of RC Component wheels for the Harley market and RC didn't want to make cruiser wheels. So with some help from a friend we started making our own line of wheels for the cruisers. The Intimidator was the first wheel we manufactured.

What about the cast vs. billet arguments. How much better is a billet wheel.

Well a cast wheel is poured, you have a mold and you pour the liquid aluminum in there and wait for it to harden. Once it hardens there are some holes left in the aluminum, some porosity. If you cut open a stock wheel, you find very small air holes.

Billet is poured too, but then it is forged into a blank and partially shaped by a process called split and spin. Between the forging and the spinning operations the pores are eliminated or greatly reduced.

Cast wheels are less expensive but the billet

This victory uses a 180X18 tire on a RC Components rim, along with matching rotor.

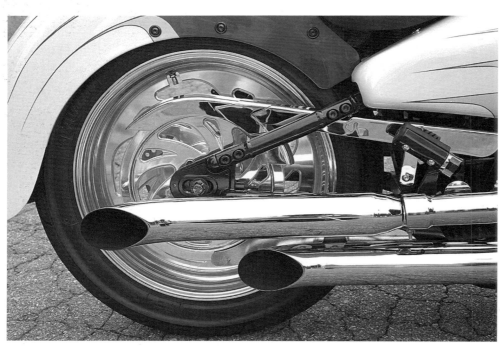

The flip side shows the matching billet pulley. Note the nice way the wheel fills the fender and how the radius of the fender matches the wheel.

wheels are much stronger, the difference is like night and day.

Can you describe the manufacture of a quality billet wheel?

We get a wheel blank from one of two companies that make them. This is the blank I already described, made from 6061 T6 aluminum. It is a formed wheel but with no hole for the axle and no spokes. These blanks come in various sizes like 16 or 17 inches in diameter and 4, 4.5 or 5 inches wide. We cut our design into the blank with our CNC equipment.

One of the hardest parts is making the hub for the rear wheel. We start off with a piece of 6061 aluminum, for some bikes the raw piece is ten inches around by ten inches thick. That piece is machined on our own CNC equipment into a hub that fits various Kawasaki, Suzuki and Yamaha models. Then it goes onto a mill where the finishing is done.

When all the machining is done both the wheels and the hubs are polished, which is one of the most expensive parts of the operation. We also offer wheels in chrome plate, so some of the parts are plated after being polished.

In the case of the rear wheels, the hub and the wheel are separate pieces?

68

Yes, that way if you bend a rim you can call and order just the wheel, which costs a lot less than the wheel and hub together.

When someone calls to ask about buying wheels for their bike, what kind of guidance do you provide to ensure they get the right wheels.

The first thing I ask them is, 'why do they want the wheels?' People laugh when I ask that. But I want to know if they're trying to customize the bike, or fix some kind of problem they're having with the bike. It could be something besides the wheel that is causing the problem and then I end up solving the problem with hours of phone calls.

Then I ask them what is it they're looking for. If the bike has a 15 inch wheel in the rear like the V-Max, our smallest is 16 inches. Do they want to change diameter? I ask what they want for width. The bike might come with a 3.5 inch wide rim but a lot of guys go to 4 or even 5 inches because they want that nice fat look in the back

Most want the stock size in front though I've had a few Kawasaki Vulcan owners who buy a 21 inch for the front and a 16X5 inch for the rear to get that Harley-Davidson Wide Glide look. The tire manufacturers recommend a 170 as the widest tire that should go on a 5 inch rim and they fit up really nice on all the bikes I've seen.

I try to make the process of buying wheels error proof. On a Suzuki, for example, we don't give them everything. We don't give them the cushion-drive but we recommend that they buy new ones and put them in. We can install them if the customer wants but it's very important that they be installed properly.

What are the mistakes people make when they buy and install new wheels on their bikes?

Most of the time when a wheel company sends out new wheels they've done lots of development and testing. Typically it's the installer who creates the problem. Out of all the sets we sold over the last year there was only one problem and we traced that back to the person who put the wheels on the bike.

Can an average person with a little mechanical knowledge put on a set of wheels at home?

First, it's a good idea to have a shop mount the tires on the rims, so you don't scratch up the rims. Then, if a person has patience and a fair amount of knowledge they can probably put the wheels on the bike as long as our shop or someone qualified installs the press-in parts. On a V-Max for example the cushion drive must be pressed in far enough, and there's also a needle bearing that should be replaced. Not all bikes are the same in terms of difficulty. The Kawasaki Vulcans are pretty easy but some others are tougher.

Some wheels come in either chrome plate or polished. Before deciding consider the rest of the bike (are your fork tubes chrome plated?) and how much cleaning and polishing you like to do.

69

Chapter Five

Brakes

Heat Machines

It's hard to discuss brakes without a parallel discussion of physics. Brakes are basically heat machines. When you squeeze the lever the brake pads are forced against the spinning rotor which slows the motorcycle. In essence you are converting the motorcycle's moving or kinetic energy into heat energy.

Kinetic energy is one of those non-linear relationships. A motorcycle traveling 60 miles per hour has four times (not two) the kinetic energy of the same machine at 30 miles per hour. When you grab a big

From Performance Machine come these high quality calipers for the Road Star. Starting at the top, a differential bore four-piston, a differential-bore six piston and a six piston designed for the rear. PM

handful of front brake at 80 or 100mph you're asking a lot of those brakes. It only makes good sense to buy the best components you can for that new motorcycle.

The nice thing about high quality brakes is the fact that they usually look as good as they work. Form follows function. The trickest calipers from Performance Machine are usually extremely functional as well. When buying brakes for a high performance motorcycle more is usually better. More rotor surface area, more pistons per caliper (usually with larger pads

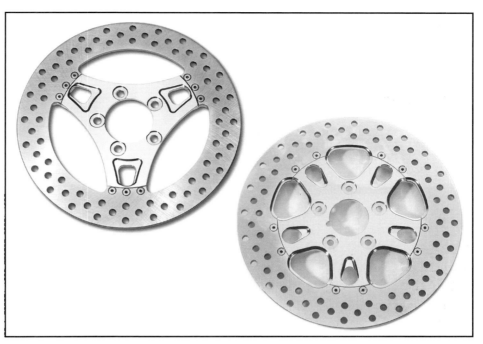

Designed to compliment the design of the wheels, these Image series rotors are available for the Road Star in stainless steel or ductile iron. PM

as well) and in some cases, more calipers. The down side to the "more brakes is better" theory is the expense, complexity and additional unsprung weight of more and bigger calipers.

THE STOCK BINDERS

Having said all that, most of the bikes that we consider cruisers come from the factory with pretty good brakes. The front is often slowed by a four piston caliper squeezing a ventilated stainless steel rotor. James at Performance Machine reports that most Metric riders are leaving the stock brakes intact, "unless they decide to buy wheels." Those new wheels (at least the ones from PM) come two ways: Designed to mate up to stock rotors and calipers, or to PM's own rotors and calipers.

Upgrades in brake performance can be had by switching to a pad with a different material. Most of these rotors are made from stainless steel, not an ideal material from a brake engineer's point of view, but very durable and tough enough that you can use almost any pad material without any danger of damaging the rotors.

Brake pads can be broken down into two types: Organic, which include Kevlar pads; and metallic, which includes sintered-iron pads. In general the metallic pads offer a higher coefficient of friction (they

Brake pads come from a number of companies in a number of different materials.

Hydraulic Ratios

How The Brakes Work

Ninety nine percent of our bikes use disc brakes operated through a hydraulic "linkage" that connects the master cylinder with the disc brake caliper(s). Essentially, when you squeeze the lever on the handle bars you displace a small volume of brake fluid and create pressure in the brake line and in the disc brake caliper. That pressure is used to force the caliper piston(s) out of their bores so the brake pad(s) are forced against the spinning rotor.

We can't move much further with this discussion without taking time to explain two very basic hydraulic laws:

1) Pressure in the brake system is equal over all surfaces of the system.

2) A fluid cannot be compressed to a smaller volume.

This means that the pressure at the master cylinder outlet is the same pressure that is applied to all the surfaces (read: caliper pistons) in the brake system. This also means the pressure at the master cylinder outlet is applied fully to the pistons and is not "used up" compressing the fluid link between the master cylinder and the calipers. The primary reason brake fluid needs a high boiling point is to prevent the liquid from turning into a gas, which is in fact a compressible material.

When you buy a new or different master cylinder you need to ensure it is matched to the other components in the system. Which brings up a short discussion of hydraulic ratios.

A demonstration of hydraulic ratios will help explain the need to correctly match the master cylinder with the calipers or wheel cylinders. The pressure of the hydraulic fluid at the master cylinder outlet is determined by that old formula from high school: Pressure = Force/Area. If you put ten pounds of force on the master cylinder piston with one square inch of area, you have created a pressure of 10psi. If however, you apply the same amount of force to a master cylinder with only 1/2 square inch of piston area, then you've created twice the pressure.

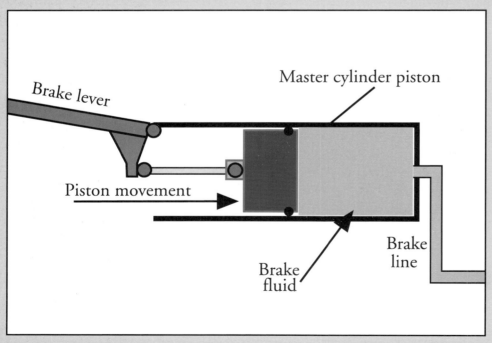

When you pull the lever, the piston displaces fluid and creates pressure within the hydraulic system. How much pressure depends on how hard you squeeze, the lever ratio, and the size of the piston.

Hydraulic Ratios

Assuming 10 psi of pressure in the line and a caliper with one square inch of piston area, the force on the brake pad will be 10 pounds (Force = Pressure X Area). If you double the piston area you also double the force on the brake pad. Thus the way to achieve maximum force on the brake pads is with a small master cylinder piston working calipers with large or multiple pistons having a high total area.

There is, as always, a trade-off in using a small diameter master cylinder piston to create more pressure. The smaller piston doesn't move as much fluid and the lever may be up against the bar when you've actually moved it far enough to displace enough fluid to push the pads against the rotor.

What's needed is a good match between the master cylinder bore diameter and the caliper(s). If in doubt ask the counter person you're buying the component from, or the manufacturer of the components for help in choosing the correct master cylinder for a particular caliper.

Anytime you open the hydraulic system for service you have to bleed the air out of the lines and calipers after the system is reassembled, lest you leave air in the lines instead of fluid. Most brake component manufacturers provide bleeding instructions and many of those like to see you "reverse bleed" the system with a small pump that forces fluid in from the bleeder screw on the caliper until the master cylinder reservoir is full. Because of the relatively small volume of fluid displaced by the master cylinder piston, this reverse method often works better than the typical automotive-based bleeding method. Repeatedly pumping up the master cylinder and then opening the bleeder screw to let the air escape doesn't work so well when the amount of brake fluid displaced is as small as it is with most motorcycle master cylinders.

The final word of warning involves safely. When the system is bled and reassembled be sure to do a thorough inspection for leaks, followed by a careful road test.

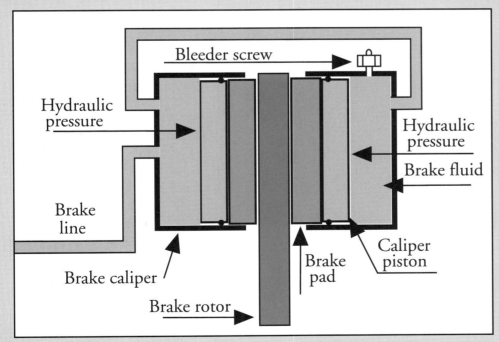

Hydraulic pressure in the caliper will force the two pistons toward the center, pushing the brake pads against the spinning rotors. More pistons (or bigger pistons) equals more area and more force.

Brake pads designed for the more popular brake rotors are often available in at least two different pad materials to better match your rotors and tastes.

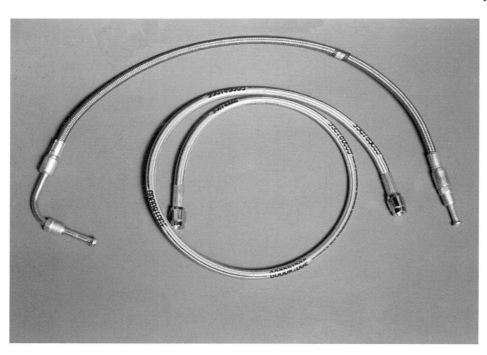

Braided stainless brake hoses are available with the ends already installed, or in a more universal form ready to accept the correct end.

grab onto the rotor more effectively at a given amount of pressure from the caliper) and work better in wet conditions.

Part of the allure of those new polished four-piston calipers is aesthetic. The stock calipers are often painted or finished in a flat aluminum finish. There are a couple of things you can do, short of buying a new caliper, that will improve the looks of the front brake set up. The easiest way to provide some additional shine without removing or replacing the caliper is with a chrome plated caliper cover, available from companies like Küryakyn or some of the manufacturers. There are also some chrome covers that stick on to the outside of the caliper. Your other option is to have the stock caliper polished to a bright shine.

BRAKE FLUID

Brake fluid is a specialized hydraulic fluid, designed to operate in a dirty environment and withstand high temperatures without boiling. When a liquid boils it becomes a gas, a compressible material, sensed by the rider as a very soft brake lever. Quality brake fluid will remain viscous at nearly any temperature and resist boiling up to 400 degrees Fahrenheit.

There are three grades of brake fluid commonly available: DOT 3, DOT 4 and DOT 5. DOT 3 and 4 are glycol-based fluids with dry boiling points of 401 and 446 degrees Fahrenheit respectively. DOT 3 and 4 fluids are hydroscopic, meaning they absorb water from the environment, and they attack most paints. DOT 5 fluid is silicone based, meaning a higher boiling point (500 degrees

Fahrenheit, dry), no tendency to absorb water and no reaction when spilled on a painted surface.

Most cruisers come from the factory with the master cylinders filled with DOT 4 fluid. While DOT 3 and DOT 4 can be mixed, you cannot mix either one with DOT 5 silicone fluid. If in doubt as to the type of fluid in your bike consult the owner's or shop manual. You can switch from one type (silicone or non-silicone) to the other but you have to completely flush the system. Remember too that because the DOT 3 and 4 fluids absorb moisture from the environment, it's a good idea to flush the system periodically per the recommendations in your owner's manual.

HOSES

Connecting the master cylinder(s) to the calipers are the flexible brake lines. Because the hydraulic pressure in the brake system approaches 1000psi you can only use hoses approved for use in hydraulic brake systems. When buying hydraulic hoses many builders use braided stainless lines from companies like Russell or Goodridge. These braided lines use Teflon inner liners to actually carry the fluid. Unlike the OEM style hoses, which may swell just slightly on a hard brake application, the Teflon liners do not expand even a little under hard braking and thus give the bike a solid feel to the lever or pedal.

Russell and Goodridge and a few others provide a variety of stainless hose styles. Most common are the universal hoses available in various lengths with a female connector attached at either end. By combining the universal hose with the right banjo bolt or connector on either end it's possible to find the right hose/ends combination for nearly any imaginable application. Notably, some of these hoses are DOT approved and some are not. This might seem like a small thing unless you live in a state with tough inspection laws.

Other differences include diameter, which comes in three sizes known as dash 2, 3 and 4, with 2 being the smallest and 3 the most common by far. If you want premade hoses without the additional hardware of a universal hose, some

catalogs and aftermarket shops stock hoses for common applications with the correct ends already installed. Your other option is to call a company like Performance Machine or Goodridge (some shops also have this capacity) with your specifications and they can make up a hose from scratch.

Goodridge makes a hose with a clear outer cover so the braid won't act like a saw if it rubs against the fender. Or you can buy shrink tubing for brake hoses and use it to coat all or part of your new stainless brake lines. The best way to ensure that the new hose won't act like a saw against that candy paint job is to route it correctly and clamp it securely with one of the many small clamps available from the aftermarket.

The threads and fittings used for brake lines and fittings are not as standardized as the threads used on common bolts and nuts. For this reason be sure you use matching components - a Russell end for a Russell hose. Many of these hoses can be used with American or Metric machines, meaning you have to ensure the banjo bolt is the right size and uses the correct threads.

If you do install those new calipers on the front fork be sure to mount the caliper so it's centered over the rotor (shims are usually provided for this purpose) and use the correct mounting brackets and bolts. The

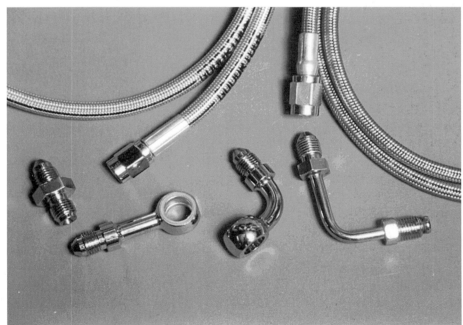

Just a small sampling of ends that are available for these dash-three hoses from Goodridge. Note that the one on the left is wrapped in plastic.

In The Shop: Caliper Installation

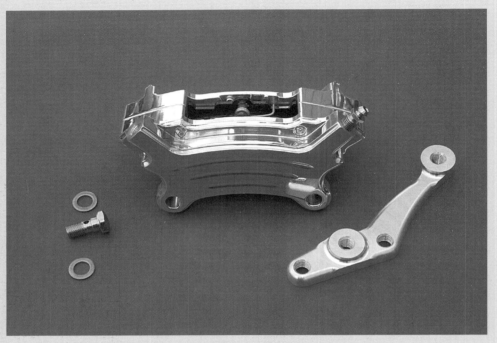

Shown here is a new caliper installation done on a Kawasaki Vulcan at the Arlen Ness facility. The caliper itself, a four piston design, is carved from billet aluminum and comes with the correct bracket. When doing work like this (or almost any other kind of work for that matter) it's a good idea to have a factory service manual for checking things like torque specifications for the various fasteners.

This new four-piston caliper (PM/Arlen Ness #02-235) comes complete with the mounting bracket and a new banjo bolt with crush washers. This is a prototype kit, the finished kits include a polished bracket.

As shown here, you don't need a lot of tools, or time, to install a new caliper like this on most bikes.

Wayne Houk, our mechanic on this job, recommends using red Loctite on the mounting bolts...

...which are then tightened with a combination wrench before being torqued to the factory specifications.

In The Shop: Caliper Installation

Now Wayne slips the caliper into position. The pads may have to be pushed back far enough so that they can slide past the rotor.

With Loctite on the threads, an Allen wrench is used to tighten the caliper-to-bracket bolts

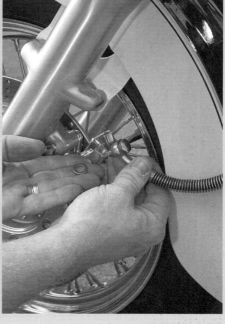

Crush washers used to seal the banjo bolts must be new, or clean and in good condition. Check for seepage after the caliper is installed.

The bleeder ends up on the bottom, so the caliper must be bled off the bike, or you need to use a reverse-bleeding pump like an EZ bleeder.

The clamp for the line (part #K-1007) is tightened in place and then bolted to the bottom of the lower triple tree.

The bracket that holds the brake line and reflector at the caliper had to be adjusted slightly, and then re-installed on the bike.

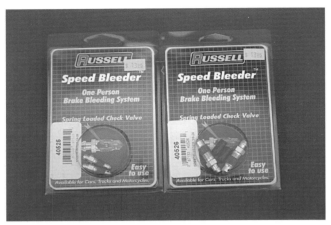

Designed to make brake bleeding a one-person operation, these bleeder screws contain a small one-way valve.

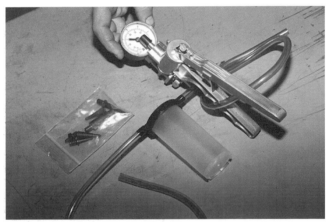

At Kokesh MC they sometimes use this kit with vacuum pump for bleeding the brakes.

Here the pump and bottle are attached to the rear caliper. The small container prevents brake fluid from filling the pump.

mounting bolts must be very high quality. Use bolts that came with the caliper kit or those that are recommended by the manufacturer.

Keep all the components matched: the right master cylinder matched to the right calipers to produce the correct pressure and travel at the lever, the right pads matched to the right rotor surface. Keep everything neat and allow no dirt or impurities into the hydraulic part of the system. If in doubt about your installation or whether or not you got all the air out of the lines, swallow your pride and ask a local shop for help.

LET IT BLEED

Anytime the hydraulic system is opened up on either end of the bike you will be forced to bleed the brakes. That is, bleed the air out of the brake system. Hydraulic brake systems work because a fluid cannot be compressed to a smaller volume – though the same cannot be said about air. If there's any air in the system the squeeze on the master cylinder lever will only compress that air, instead of creating useful hydraulic pressure.

In the case of the old Chevy in the garage, the normal bleeding procedure (the most common one anyway) is to fill the master cylinder with fluid, install the cap and have a helper pump the mushy brake pedal. Then while they hold the pedal to the floor you open the bleeder screw. Each time the bleeder screw is opened a little spurt of air and brake fluid escapes. The trick is to close the bleeder *before* the helper lets the pedal pop up.

By doing this repeatedly fresh brake fluid is forced from the master cylinder to the caliper and eventually out the bleeder screw. Any air is pushed out of the bleeder ahead of the fluid. The project is done when the pedal is rock-hard, and fresh brake fluid with no sign of air comes out the bleeder each time it is opened. If, during all this pumping and bleeding, the pedal (or lever) is allowed to snap back while the bleeder is still open air is pulled back *into* the caliper.

Though you can follow the same methods for bleeding the brakes on your V-Star the results don't always work as well. The biggest problem is the small size of the master cylinder piston. There simply isn't much fluid displaced on each stroke. As my mechanic-friend Patrick explains the problem, "With the little master cylinder it takes a long time to move that bubble of air from the master cylinder to the bleeder screw."

Motorcycles have a couple of additional problems. One is best stated by Elmer, long-time mechanic at Kokesh MC in Spring Lake Park, Minnesota. "If the shape of the handle bars has the master cylinder pointing uphill, then you get a bubble of air in the line right where it connects to the master cylinder. That's the highest point in the system so it's almost impossible to get rid of that bubble. You have to lean the bike over so the master points downhill, or take the master cylinder off the bars and point it downhill.

The other potential problem is the way aftermarket calipers sometimes mount with the bleeder screw at the bottom of the caliper. Air always rises so with the bleeder at the bottom you can't really bleed the caliper of air. The solution is to take the caliper off the bracket and hold it so the bleeder is at the top. Then put something between the pads and then get on with the bleeding.

Though this all sounds simple enough more than one intrepid motorcycle mechanic has failed to get all the air out of the brake system. A variety of devices are sold to make the job easier. Some, like the EZ-Bleeder, force fluid in at the bleeder and then through the line to the master cylinder until the reservoir is full and the system is purged of air. The mechanics we spoke with, including John at JAZ and Elmer at Kokesh, both prefer bleeding machines that attach to the bleeder and then suck the fluid from the reservoir to and through the bleeder (see the photos for examples of this style of bleeding aid).

If you've never bled brakes before you might want to stop at the local scooter shop and buy one of the bleeding devices that they recommend. "Some bikes are just really hard to bleed," explains John from JAZ Cycle. "Especially bikes with integrated braking systems like the new 1800 Honda. Sometimes you have to just take it to the shop and let them do it with something like the power bleeder we have."

No matter how you bleed the brakes, do not settle for a spongy pedal or lever. And be sure to inspect all the junctions for leaks with the system under pressure. Finally, remember that brake fluid eats paint, and that more than very small amounts of used fluid should be saved and taken to your county recycling center.

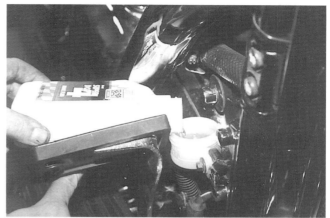

A simple bleeding sequence at JAZ cycle, starts by filling the master cylinder (be sure to keep it full).

John cracks the the bleeder screw loose before he starts bleeding.

With a commercial bleeding pump attached John opens the bleeder until there is pure fluid and no sign of air coming out of the caliper.

Dream Bikes

There are a least a thousand different ways to personalize your motorcycle. While there may be no right or wrong when it comes time to make that two-wheeled machine in the garage better fit your personality, some ideas are simply better than others.

The idea here is to look at what other people have done and let those owners share their stories with a wider audience. All so that you can learn from the successes and occasional mistakes of your peers.

The bikes represent a variety of brands, styles and budgets. Some are simple and some are complex. Each is one rider's Dream Bike.

Jeff Irwin, 1998 Aero

Jeff Irwin elected to go with the, nostalgic, 1950s, low-rider, tail-dragger, theme, "because that's the way the bike starts off from the factory. I chose to keep the factory wire wheels and the white side-wall tires because they work with the theme."

In order to lower the back of the bike more than the front, Jeff called Progressive Suspension, who made up a special set of ten inch canister shocks for the Aero. In front, Jeff used a Progressive spring kit to shorten the fork two inches. When Jeff did his customizing the chrome side covers were not available from Honda, so he had his covers dipped in the chrome tank. At the same time all the aluminum on the bike was removed, polished and reinstalled.

To hide the radiator Jeff installed an air dam from Corbin. The same company contributed a tan, ostrich covered solo seat. The mirrors seen on the bike are from Arlen Ness, though the grips are from Highway

Jeff Irwin took the term "tail dragger" literally, by lowering the back of his bike more than the front - all part of the old-time hot rod theme he chose for his Honda Aero.

The air dam from Corbin does a good job of hiding the Honda's radiator. Despite the air dam, most of the equipment on this bike is stock, including the sheet metal, black paint, and wire wheels.

Hawk. A variety of small items help to further brighten the bike, like the chrome driveshaft cover and the triple tree covers from Aeromach. Jeff wanted to keep the bike "really clean looking," so he stayed with the factory black paint.

To help out in the horsepower department without spending too much cash, Jeff gutted the factory pipe, installed a K&N airbox kit and had the carb rejetted.

Instead of creating a new theme Jeff chose to enhance the styling cues created by the factory. The result is a good looking bike done without so much as a new paint job.

Holland Powell, 1988 Vulcan Classic

Holland Powell's pride and joy started life as a bone-stock 1998 Kawasaki Vulcan Classic. "I had bikes when I was younger," explains Holland. "Then I got into cars. The last one was a turbo Porsche, but when my daughter turned 16 the insurance went right through the roof." The Kawasaki took over that holy place in the garage. An employee benefits specialist by day, Holland spends his evenings tinkering with the Vulcan.

The big Classic came in basic black, a color that painter Ken Lawrence used as the basecoat for the flames. Though the body of the flames are done in platinum the licks are done in special chameleon paint that changes color depending on the type and angle of light. Before painting the rear fender, Holland removed the stock lights, had the holes filled and then installed an Arlen Ness light and turn signal assembly. Because he didn't like the leather bags that came with the bike Holland replaced them with the hard bags seen here, painted to match the rest of the bike. And instead of laying out big bucks for billet wheels, Holland chose to use the chrome wheel covers from Custom World International.

The 1500cc Vulcan gets extra power from an airbox kit, a re-jetted carburetor and a pair of Vance & Hines pipes. The flamed cover seen on the air cleaner is a good example of what an owner can do with a little creativity. "That cover is what they call a derby cover for a Harley-Davidson," says Holland.

Big and bright pretty well describes this Vulcan Classic. Rather than completely repaint the bike, Holland chose to have the flames laid on right over the stock factory black paint.

If the paint alone isn't bright enough, Holland also added a light bar and Arlen Ness taillight assembly. To make it easier to stretch out while riding Holland added forward controls and floor boards.

"I bought it and used it as the cover for the air box."

Other bright spots include the chrome side covers, the mini ape-hanger bars on two inch risers and the Arlen Ness mirrors. The windshield is a thirteen inch model from Minnesota Fats and came with the small stash pouch seen on the inside.

Extra chrome bits include the filler panel seen behind the rear cylinder (new home for the ignition switch) and the cover for the drive-shaft housing. Even the stock seat had to be replaced with a studded model from Travelcade.

Dream Bikes

Dennis Donnelly, 1998 Intruder 1500

Known to friends as Vito, Dennis Donnelly was looking at Royal Stars when he happened to sit on a slightly used Suzuki Intruder in a dealer's lot. Sitting on the bike felt like slipping on a his favorite pair of blue jeans and Dennis knew the Intruder was the bike for him.

After riding it stock for one season Dennis decided to make a few changes. "My wife thought I was crazy," recalls Dennis. "But I tore the whole thing apart and took the tank, fenders and side covers to a fella in town, a second-generation painter, and told him 'I like green.'"

When Dennis reassembled the bike he added all the chrome accessories he could find, which wasn't many. What he could find came from the Suzuki dealer, including the windshield and a series of chrome covers. New seat designs aren't real prevalent for the Suzuki either, so Dennis had the original seat redone with gel inserts and new upholstery chosen to match the colors used in the paint.

At the end of his second season, Dennis again tore the Suzuki apart. This time the swingarm and driveshaft housing went out for chrome plating. Dennis also installed a pair of Hard Chrome pipes and then had the dealer re-jet the carburetor to give his Suzy a bit more snort when the light turns green.

Dennis, who makes his living as a dental technician at a lab in St. Louis, is pretty happy with the Intruder. "I could have a Harley for about the same money," says Dennis, "but not with all the extras I've done. I thought of if as a 'best buy' when I bought it and it's only gotten better with the changes I've made."

A lot of customizers say "paint makes the bike" and that's certainly the case for this big Intruder.

Just because there aren't very many accessories available for the big Suzuki Intruder, doesn't mean you can't improve the looks of the bike with paint, a reupholstered seat and a few accessories.

Dennis rode motorcycles as a kid, but was without a two-wheeled conveyance for some time. Since the Suzuki came along Dennis spends summers riding and winters improving.

Dream Bikes

Jimmy Creasy, Honda Valkyrie.

A big hulking motorcycle has at least one advantage over a smaller, machine. The size brings with it plenty of surface area. Think of it as a canvas upon which the owner can express his or her personality.

Jimmy Creasy from Creasy's Honda in Lexington, Tennessee chose to use the ample surface provided by his Valkyrie touring rig to express his long-standing fascination with NASCAR racing. "I pulled all the sheet metal off," explains Jimmy, "and took it to Chris Cruise in Deland, Florida. I gave Chris pretty explicit instructions as to what I wanted, and I've worked with him before so there weren't any surprises." Before taking the fender to Chris, Jimmy removed the stock tail-light assembly and replaced it with a Harley taillight and an Arlen Ness mini light bar.

It takes more than great paint to create a bright stunning motorcycle. In Jimmy's case that extra shine comes from things like the chrome plated wheels, brake calipers and rearend housing. Jimmy's big six cylinder also benefits from the more typical additions. Things like the chrome rails that wrap around the bags and the chrome engine covers. There are plenty of smaller bits of brightness as well, some that you can't even see unless you look up under the bike. According to Jimmy, "all the chrome goodies came either from Honda or Cobra."

Most Valkyries don't need help in the power department, but that didn't stop Jimmy from advancing the timing an extra six degrees, adding Cobra pipes (with baffles) and installing a new jet

Jimmy Creasy started customizing bikes when the 450 Hondas came out way back when. Today he runs Creasy's Honda where they personalize a lot of bikes for their customers.

The paint on this Honda isn't just busy, it's very bright. The red base paint combined with the abundant chrome make this one Honda that has viewers reaching for their dark glasses.

kit in each of the six carburetors. Though the front of the bike rides at stock height, the rear is slightly lower due to the shorter shocks installed at Jimmy's shop.

Jimmy didn't miss much when he customized the big Honda. Nearly all the cables and brake lines have been swapped for braided replacements. The handle bars support aftermarket grips and Arlen Ness mirrors with built in turn signals.

Big and bright, Jimmy Creasy's Valkyrie is a good reflection of his personal passion, and a bike you won't see duplicated any time soon.

Dream Bikes

Sterling Winters, 1994 Suzuki 1400 cc Intruder

From the 36 degree rake angle to the king and queen seat, the 1400 cc Intruder comes stock with a strong chopper flavor. When Sterling Winters modified his Intruder he chose to move away from that image without doing any radical surgery.

The biggest part of Sterling's transformation from chopper to modern cruiser is the addition of a new gas tank. "The tank came from the Fat Tank Company in California," explains Sterling, "They take a Harley Fat Bob tank and modify it to set down onto the top tube instead of sitting up on top of the tube like the stock one does."

The other key to the personality change is the deletion of the stock front wheel. The tall skinny chopper wheel made a trip to Buchanans Spoke and Rim, where a sixteen by three and a half inch rim was laced up to the stock hub. The new wider tire meant Sterling had to "widen" the front fork assembly with new wider triple trees from Highway Hawk.

Other changes to the sheet metal include a new front fender from Sumax with a flipped trailing lip. The rear fender is from Cobra, though Sterling had to reshape the trailing edge to better match the shape of the front fender. At the back of the fender Sterling installed a tombstone taillight.

The bike is about an inch and a half lower than stock, accomplished in front with the smaller diameter front wheel, and in back with a pair of shorter progressive shock absorbers. Perhaps the final change in the Intruder's personality is the conversion to a solo seat.

Sterling Winters kept the clean and sanitary style of his 1400 Intruder yet completely changed the bike's personality. Abundant chrome includes the front frame cover and the fork's lower legs.

Sterling likes the bike's small oil cooler (instead of a big radiator). Note the small aftermarket turn signals in back and the rather short shock absorbers. The converted tank, flipped front fender and tombstone taillight gives the bike a strong Harley feel.

Eliminating the passenger pillion meant relocating the relays that normally reside under that part of the seat.

Engine upgrades are a little hard to find for the Suzuki line. Sterling did rejet the carburetor with a kit from Cobra, add a new Dyna ignition module and a Rifle exhaust system.

Sterling, who makes his living as a Jeep mechanic, thinks the best part of customizing a metric cruiser is the way it makes him, "feel like a pioneer" because there aren't many parts available for the metric bikes.

Ken Lee, 1999 Victory V92C

Ken Lee, a Victory dealer from Inman, South Carolina, built the bike seen here to draw attention to both the bike and his shop. "I wanted to draw attention," says Ken, "but I didn't want to spend a ton of money to do it."

Most of the money Ken did spend went into the RC Component wheels and the multi-colored paint job. Matt Sanders from Spartanburg, South Carolina created the multi-colored scalloped paint job. Not only does the paint add to the bike's visual impact, the horizontal lines that Ken incorporated into the design help to stretch out the bike and make it look longer and lower than it really is.

The wheels are from RC Components and measure sixteen inches in front and eighteen in the rear. A Dunlop 130 series tire wraps the front rim while a fat 180 is used in the rear. "I chose the eighteen in back so you would see more wheel and less tire," explains Ken. "The 180 tire is about as wide as you can go. It fits the fender well and doesn't rub, but anything wider probably would." Ken chose to use matching rotors, also from RC Components. Ken's final comments on the wheels involve the way they fit, "they just go right in with no hassles and no extra spacers."

The bike does sit two inches closer to the asphalt than a stocker. To lower his Victory Ken modified the rear shock, and then slid the fork tubes up in the triple trees. The slim seat from Corbin works well with Ken's sleek and low theme. Extra

Ken Lee's Victory is another example of how much you can change a bike with only paint, wheels and a few accessories.

Victory dealers sell Arlen Ness accessories, which Lee used to good effect. The rest of the bike is defined by the RC wheels, which came with matching rotors and rear wheel pulley.

trim includes the rear light assembly from Arlen Ness, along with Ness mirrors and grips

Ken says that most Victory customers who come into his shop leave their bikes pretty much stock - until they see what he's done with the Victory seen here. Then they want to know how they can make their bike look like that bright one parked in front of the store.

The best thing about the bike, says Ken, "is the fact that all the parts, with the exception of the wheels, are available direct from your Victory dealer."

Dream Bikes

Sandralee Watters, 1998 Honda Shadow A.C.E.

We caught up with Sandralee Watters at the Honda Hoot in Asheville, North Carolina, one of her stops in a six month exploration of America. "I love hot pink," is how she explains the most obvious change she's made to her Honda A.C.E. touring rig. In fact, the original color the painter sprayed wasn't quite bright enough, so she asked for a pearl over-lay "for more sparkle."

Considering the attention to detail displayed in the bike and the paint work, it's not too surprising to learn that Sandralee is an artist working in various media from computers to clay. The design on the tank is based on a tattoo on Sandralee's shoulder though the airbrush artist used an image of the endangered Florida Panther as the template for the feline face that stares out from the flowers. Both the hot pink and the graphic designs are the work of Irby Designs in Watsonville, California. The paw prints scattered through the paint job are matched by the prints stitched into the seat cover by the cooperative crew at the Corbin seat facility.

Complimenting the bright paint are some additional chrome covers and guards. From the Cobra catalog Sandralee ordered floorboards, a front lightbar, the case guards, a radiator cover and the brake pedal cover. A Hondaline rack made it possible to mount the Givi top box.

"I didn't do much mechanically with the bike," explains Sandralee, "because I like the sound, the size of the engine and the way she feels." Sandralee goes on to explain that, "the bike is a reflection of my personality. It's flamboyant and I've been accused of being

More artist than mechanic, it's not surprising that Sandralee should personalize her bike with paint and graphics, rather than new sheet metal or too many chrome accessories.

Call it graphics or air-brush work, designs like this fall into two categories: very good or very, very bad. This example works because of the high quality work, the tasteful design and the way it all comes together on the bike.

flamboyant. This is definitely my motorcycle. I've had comments that the bike is 'over the top', but it isn't even close yet."

Further modifications to the bright pink A.C.E. aren't likely however, as an accident in Michigan left Sandralee with two broken arms and a crumpled Honda. If a silver lining can be found to such a painful event, it came as she had her first post-surgical conference with the doctor. When the doctor entered the hospital room there was only one thing Sandralee wanted to know, "when can I ride again?" She's now looking for a new motorcycle.

Todd Stoop, 1998
1500 Vulcan Classic

Todd Stoop customized "Big Red" twice, and the lessons he learned along the way bear repeating.

Todd bought the 1500 Kawasaki, "because it seemed like the best bike for the money and there were plenty of aftermarket parts." The fixing up started with standard add-ons and paint. An Aeromach license plate bracket and a cover for the air cleaner. From the same company Todd purchased a set of billet mirrors and new hand grips for the ends of the handle bars.

To lower the bike about two inches Todd purchased shorter shocks and a fork lowering kit from Progressive. At the same time he decided to install a pair of chrome lower legs from Kawasaki's Fire and Steel catalog. A studded solo seat from Corbin and a little airbrush work on the side covers made the bike look like a real custom. Thus equipped Todd took it to Daytona for the first time.

"After being in Daytona," explains Todd, "I decided the bike was almost too much. I learned that you have to pick a theme instead of just buying stuff and hanging it on the bike. So I tore it all apart again and sent the sheet metal to my brother Art, who works at Kinetic Art in West Palm Beach, Florida. He and I decided on straight red paint. We figured it's a bright color that shows off the chrome the way a black velvet background shows off a piece of jewelry."

At the same time Todd took the seat pan from the solo seat to an upholstery shop and had it done

"Just Say No" might be Todd's slogan for the second round of customizing on his Big Red Kawasaki. No extra chrome and no graphics to create a bike the he calls "truly unique."

Todd said yes to some nice mechanical details like the Russell braided lines. The aftermarket parts on the bike are chrome because Todd doesn't like the maintenance that polished parts require.

in tan leather, with a matching strip that runs down the center of the gas tank. Todd bought solid wheel covers that give the look of billet without the high cost. While he was at it Todd decided to let his brother Art (a mechanic as well as a painter) install high compression pistons, new Muzzy camshafts and a pair of Vance and Hines pipes.

"When I got it all together the second time it flowed really nice," says Todd. "I wanted something you couldn't just go out and buy the parts for and that's what I have. I learned that you can spend money and not get results that you like."

Dream Bikes

1998 Valkyrie, FDR Kawasaki

When Mark from FDR Kawasaki started on the Valkyrie seen here he wanted to create a custom bike that, "would fit my personal style." In creating his personal statement Mark used a number of accessories that aren't normally seen on a Honda. "We used parts from Arlen Ness, Drag Specialties and Pro One that are really meant for the Harley line," says Mark. Examples include the long sexy Arlen Ness headlight and the cat's-eye taillight that fits up under the fat bob rear fender from Drag Specialties.

The widest rear fender they could find in the fat bob style was a little over eight inches wide. Mark and his crew bought the too-narrow fender, cut it in half, bolted each half to the stock fender struts and then clamped sheet metal into the missing center section. Then the whole thing was taken to the local body shop. They in turn cut a center strip of the right dimension, welded it into the gap and finished the whole thing off with a little bondo and plenty of black paint.

Under the fender resides a very wide 200X16 inch tire mounted to the stock Honda wheel. Up front mark used a low profile 120X17 inch tire to both lower the front end and give the bike that racy stance he was looking for. The two things that really lock in that drag-bike feel however, are the Nitrous Express system and the shortened six into six Cobra exhaust system.

Additional accents include the flat drag bars from Flanders (because all the Honda cruisers use one-inch bars, handle bars and accessories meant for

Some people would say a Valkyrie is too big to be a good hot rod. One look at Mark's hot six cylinder proves otherwise.

This bike has all the right visual cues: The NOS bottle, fat rear tire, six into six pipes and velocity stacks. They all add up to make a big Honda with an even bigger attitude. Note the Aeromach bullets on the ends of the fork tubes.

Harley-Davidsons can be easily used) with grips from Jardine. Velocity stacks from Aeromach tie in nicely with the performance theme. The bike is lowered through the use of shorter Works Performance shock absorbers, made up special for this bike, and the lower profile front tire. More shine comes from the polished rims and the numerous covers from Honda and Cobra. All in all it's one very fast, very bad looking Valkyrie, created without chopping the frame or disassembling the engine.

Husband & Wife Yamaha V-Twins

When it comes to motorcycles, Gerri and James wood have a lot in common. Husband and wife, both ride Yamaha V-Twins and both use the paint job by Alton Jones from Columbia, South Carolina as the main attraction.

Though it's true Gerri converted her factory seat to solo use and added the light bar and a hundred small bolt covers and other accents, the one thing that distinguishes her Yamaha V-Star from all the other Stars in the parking lot is the dripping paint with highlights in blue topaz (Gerri's favorite color) and jade green. Performance upgrades include a pair of aftermarket pipes and a re-jetted carburetor. Gerri says that once she and the painter decided on the design and the colors the project took on "a life of its own."

Husband James pulled the tank off his Road Star almost as soon as he got the bike home. "I really like the lines on the tank as it comes down around the seat," explains James. "I think it makes the bike look really sleek." The stretched tank also creates a nice canvas for paint work. Though in case that isn't enough area, Jim eliminated the stock taillight assembly and license plate bracket so the back fender could become "a place for art work." Jim moved the turn signals to the fender struts and the license plate to a side-mount bracket mounted on the left side.

The installation of a stretched tank with wild paint made James Road Star an instant "custom." Drag pipes and side-mount license plate bracket only add icing to the cake.

When Gerri bought her V-Star 1100 it was painted silver "and had no personality whatsoever." The new paint, a solo seat, and plenty of small pieces provide all the personality it lacked before — and then some.

Additional upgrades include the straight pipes, a rejetted carburetor, and a variety of chrome pieces like the new brake pedal and the skull on the sissy bar with eyes that come on with the taillight. The paint itself might be called skulls in the abstract. "Some people don't even realize those are skulls, it's all so stylized," says James. Skulls or not, the flowing design, the stretched tank, and the long pipes all work together to create one long, unique Road Star.

Chapter Seven

The Importance of Paint

Spray-On Personality

For anyone who intends to go past the point of just bolting a few chrome accessories to their bike, there is one question more important than any other. Actually this is a series of questions, each one interconnected. The question: What to do with the paint?

The paint job can literally make or break the project. In terms of "bang for the buck" you get a better return from a well-chosen basic paint job than any other single modification. A mild custom machine made up of nothing more than a nice sim-

This Kawasaki is a very nice, very radical bike complete with custom fenders and plenty of chrome and accessories. But when you first see the bike, what you "see" isn't the trick fenders what you see is the wild paint job.

ple paint job and some well chosen accessories can often outshine a much more expensive machine with elaborate paint laid over modified sheet metal.

If the goal of this bike building project is to have a personalized bike, one you don't see in every parking lot or dealer showroom, the easiest way to accomplish that goal is with a paint job.

It doesn't have to be wild or terribly expensive (though good paint doesn't come cheap). The paint job you choose does need to match the rest of the modifications you're making to the bike. There is nothing wrong with a single color. Sometimes less is more. The goal should be something that reflects your personality, your design goals for the new machine. Don't assume you need to have flames or graphics or a bright multi-colored tie-died pattern.

Simple paint jobs have the advantage of being less expensive. They also allow for further evolution later. You can start with solid red like Todd Stoop did with his Kawasaki (see Dream Bikes) and then add more pinstripes or graphics later. Remember that a solid color can be enhanced with simple stripes or gold leaf or graphics laid right on top.

These accents can be added right after the paint job, or later. After you've had time to look over the bike in its new color and carefully consider what color(s) might really make the whole thing jump. When it comes to paint, it's easier to add than subtract.

Flames never go away and never go out of style. These white flames with long overlapping licks jump right off the bike.

A more traditional set of flames, red on yellow, with licks on the seat.

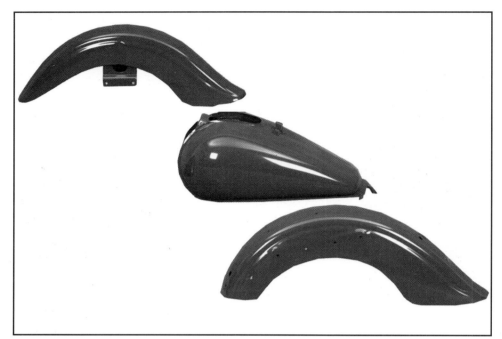

The complete sheet metal sets from Kawasaki come in primer ready to paint, or already painted in a limited range of colors and designs. Kawasaki

KAWASAKI CUSTOM TANK AND FENDER SETS

For years Harley-Davidson dealers have offered custom painted sheet metal for their most popular models. It's an easy way to customize the bike without the hassle of disassembly and the waiting while the painter takes his or her sweet time to do the paint work. It's also a nice way to create the convertible effect.

Kawasaki has a similar program that takes most of the pain out of a painting project. Just trot down to the dealer and check out their already painted fenders and tanks for the Vulcan. Ready to paint fenders and tanks are also available for the Vulcan, with a gray basecoat already applied, so you don't have to strip and paint the sheet metal on your bike.

CHEATING – HOW TO GET A COMPLETE PAINT JOB WITHOUT REALLY TRYING

If you don't own a Vulcan or you simply don't want to remove the sheet metal from the bike for any reason, there is a short cut to obtaining a custom paint job on your cruiser. As seen in the In The Shop sequence in this chapter, a bike that comes stock in one color or mostly one color can have a new graphics job laid on right over the factory paint. Many of the new Honda models for example come in black. You can totally change the look of your Valkyrie or Shadow by adding flames, pinstripes or panels, right over the stock paint.

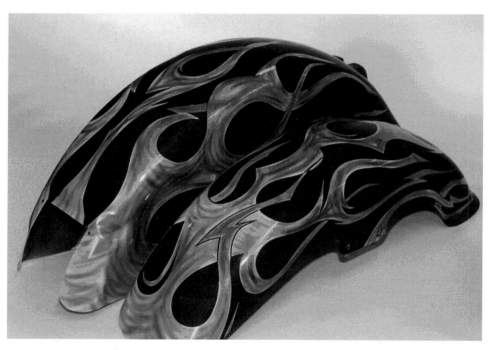

Seen at Wizard Custom Studios before application of the clearcoat, this set of sheet metal displays some very wild multi-colored flames.

The latest flame designs are evolving away from the traditional into a tribal form.

At any big show the various airbrush artists have their tents and trailers set up. In only an afternoon you can have paint added to one fender or the entire bike. Each of these painters has at least one big photo file of their favorite bikes. These books work as idea generators for potential customers. They also serve to give potential customizers a good idea of the artist's work and his or her strong points.

There is nothing wrong with this approach, though there are a few pitfalls. The first potential problem is time. In the rush of the event and the constraints put on you by a painter with only three days to do fifteen or thirty paint jobs, you might not take enough time to pick the very best design. A better approach would be to have a good idea what you want before going to the event. Then spend your time leafing through the photo notebooks until you find an artist who's good at doing the type of work you have in mind. If you want flames, find someone who does really, really nice flames. If you want the

ever-popular eagle, then find the painter with the most life-like eagles in the sample file.

The second potential pitfall is the fact that most of these painters don't clearcoat the newly applied graphics or stripes. The reasons many don't clearcoat the designs has to do with time, and the fact that a good clearcoat requires at least some kind of token paint booth. The booth helps keep the paint fumes from overwhelming any of the vendor's neighbors and minimizes dust that might become imbedded in the new paint while it's still wet.

The clearcoat, while not essential, will add to the shine, help protect the new designs from everyday nicks and gas spills, and also provide a measure of UV protection.

THE FLAMED VALKYRIE

In order to provide some insight into the work that goes into a complete paint job, we've included a

Front view of the Valkyrie project bike with flames done in greens and blues.

93

start to finish paint job on a Honda Valkyrie with after-market bags and fairing. The work is done by Bruce Bush at Wizard Custom Studios in Blaine, Minnesota. Rather than provide a lengthy explanation of the processes we've decided to let the photos and captions tell most of the story. Because the intent here is to help you appreciate the process rather than make you a painter, we've gone light on the technical details like mixing ratios and spray patterns.

Based on the 650 Star, this Yamaha project bike was built in part to show what a nice bike a small cruiser can be. The bike also illustrates the point that what separates a custom cruiser from all the other bikes is the paint.

INSIDE THE PAINT CAN

Even if you don't intend to shoot your own paint job it helps to understand the different types of paints, and the advantages and disadvantages of each. With this knowledge you can better choose the best paint for your bike, and speak with the painter in his or her own lingo. What follows is a short explanation of enamels and lacquers, primers, candys and clearcoats.

In the days before there were any "Metric cruisers," choosing a paint was pretty easy. There were enamels and nitrocellulose lacquers in a rather limited range of colors. Today there are at least three types of finish paints in a bewildering array of colors, not to mention special finishes like metallics, pearls and candy colors. Making sense of all this is easier if we first break the paint down to its basic components, and then discuss the three basic types of paint.

Despite the fact that they can be easier to use than the urethanes, lacquers are being phased out of most paint lines due to VOC and durability issues

A creative painter can use raw flake, available in a number of sizes and colors, to mix totally unique paint.

are known in the industry as VOCs and have come under government regulation. These VOCs react with sunlight and can be a major contributor to smog. In order to reduce VOCs, most current paints have a higher percentage of solids than a similar product produced only a few years ago.

THE THREE MAJOR TYPES OF PAINT

Most of the paints available for painting your Cruiser can be classified as either a lacquer, an enamel or a urethane. Though ure-

First, the paint, any paint, is made up of three basic components: pigment, resin and solvent, as well as a few additives.

Pigment is the material that gives the paint its color. Older paints often used lead-based pigments while modern paints have converted to non-lead pigments. Resin (also known as Binder) helps to hold the pigments together and keep them sticking to the metal. Solvent is the carrier used to make the paint thin enough to spray. In the case of lacquers a true thinner is used while in the case of an enamel the solvent is a reducer. Additives are materials added to the paint to give it a certain property or help it overcome a problem much the way that additives are incorporated into modern oils to improve their performance.

If we're going to talk about paint, then there are a few more terms to get out of the way. One that crops up more and more is VOCs, or Volatile Organic Compounds. Another related term is solids, as in, "high-solids" paint.

Going back to the three basic components of paint, the solvent (a volatile material) evaporates (or oxidizes) after the paint is sprayed on the bike leaving behind the pigment and binder, known as the solids. Solvents that evaporate into the atmosphere

Most big paint companies have paint systems that include basecoats (paint that is not catalyzed with isocyanates) which are then topcoated with one or more coats of urethane.

Shop Time: Paint Without Pain

A heat gun (or heavy duty hair dryer) helps convince the adhesive to let go so the panels can be peeled off.

Elbow grease is used here in lieu of solvents to remove the last of the adhesive.

With the tank cleaned up it's time to mask off the area that will be painted.

Illustrated and explained here is a start to finish graphics paint job done on a motorcycle without removing the sheet metal. The work is being performed to a new 1100 Yamaha V Star owned by Tammie Newell. The Graphics are the work of Bert Ballowe with help from his assistant Sheryl Ballowe. The work was performed during the Honda Hoot festivities in Asheville, North Carolina.

Sheryl starts the job by taking off the tank emblems. "Some of these have pins on the back side that you can't see," explains Sheryl, "and after you take off the emblem there are two holes in the tank." On this bike though the emblems are glued on and they come off pretty easy, it's a new bike, I can tell it hasn't been out in the sun very much. I use a heat gun and peel them off carefully. Then, to get off the adhesive I try to just peel it off. If you use adhesive remover it can leave behind contaminants that will mess with the paint job we do, causing fish-eyes and such. Lacquer thinner turns it into a gooey mess. After I have the adhesive off the tank I prepare the area with wax and grease remover, to remove any wax and traces of adhesive."

Next, Sheryl masks off the parts of the tank that will not be painted. They are going to work within the light panel on the sides of the tank. "I work right up to the edge of the factory tape line," explains Sheryl. "Fine line tape is what I use at the edge, then regular masking tape for the rest of the tank. It's important to use 3M tape because it's going to be on there for awhile. Some of the cheaper tapes will leave adhesive behind."

Now Sheryl finishes masking off the rest of the bike and the engine, "for the clearcoat I will mask off the whole bike, but for the graphic work on the tank this partial masking is good enough." After the tank and engine are masked off, Sheryl uses a green Scotch-Brite pad to scuff the surface. "I rub until you can't see any shiny paint anymore. Otherwise when he paints the clear, the clear won't stick."

It's important that the scuffing be done right

Shop Time: Paint Without Pain

up to the edge of the tape. Sheryl uses a "prep pen", a small "pen" with an abrasive stick inside. Though she says you can also do it with your finger nail and a Scotch-Brite pad.

Now she wipes it down with Prepsol (a pre-paint cleaner that leaves no residue behind) before starting the actual painting. "The Prepsol gets rid of finger prints," explains Sheryl, "things that will cause trouble later with the adhesion of the clearcoat."

At this point, Bert applies transfer paper, this is computer transfer paper that is one layer thick, some are multi-layer. Before starting Bert explains his favorite technique. "I like to draw out the

design, instead of doing it with tape. That way I can see the design before I start painting. Then if I like it I cut it out. The nice thing about doing it this way is you have the piece you cut out, you can put that back down later and use it to mask over one part of the design while you paint another part, or you can cover the whole design before you paint in a background.

Bert slits the paper and works it over the tank with his fingernails, explaining, "the trouble with the paper is it can be hard to get it to lay flat on the curved surface." From here the project moves quickly through a series of steps:

Bert draws out the design on the transfer

Sheryl uses a Scotch-Brite pad to knock down the paint's gloss and create a surface that fresh paint will adhere to.

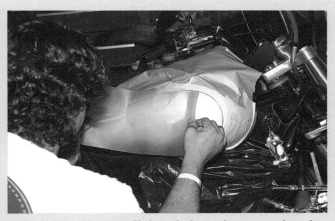

After the tank is scuffed and cleaned Bert applies the transfer paper.

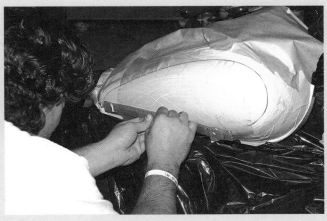

The design is drawn out on the paper then each section is cut out separately.

Shop Time: Paint Without Pain

At this stage Bert has already pulled out one piece of the design and started to paint.

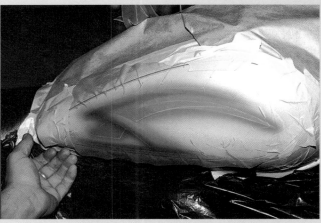

At this point the basic design is finished, though there's some important detail work left.

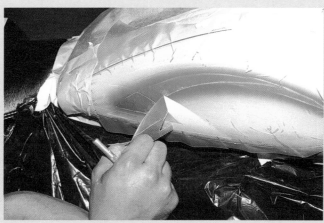

After replacing the first piece of paper so it acts as a mask, Bert pulls out another piece of the design....

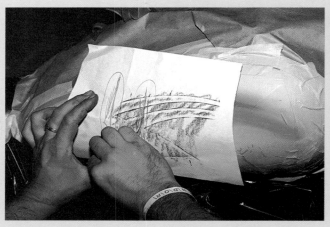

With a piece of charcoal and a sheet of paper Bert is able to make a simple template of the design.

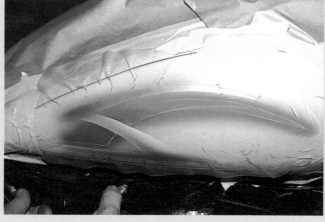

....and applies a different shade of paint to the second spear.

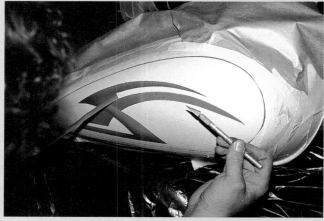

As Bert pulls away the transfer paper the design emerges.

Shop Time: Paint Without Pain

paper, using a rough sketch he and the customer agreed upon as his guide. Next, he cuts out part of the design, just one spear and pulls that part out of the transfer paper. Time to begin painting. Bert paints in the first spear using maroon, then orange then a third color. These are all done with Shimrin base coats from House of Kolor.

Next, Bert puts the original spear of paper back down to act as a mask before moving on.

Now he pulls additional paper for more of the design, and applies another color. Obviously a lot of variation is possible here, as in the number of paint shadings and the complexity of the design.

With a dark charcoal stick and a piece of paper, Bert creates a template (see photo) of the design, one that can be used on the other side of the tank. Almost done, Bert pulls the rest of the transfer paper, and cleans up any overspray with reducer.

Now Bert uses fine line tape to enhance the design, explaining, "the tape is easier to use sometimes than trying to cut the design out of the transfer paper."

After painting the lines and pulling that tape, it's time for the shadows. "The shadows are real important," explains Bert. "The best trick I know to really add dimension to the design. The shadows really make it pop."

To transfer the design to the other side, Bert pieces together the cut out pieces from the right side, puts them on the left, over the transfer paper on that side of the tank, then applies a dusting of dark paint that will leave a line. Then he removes the pieces from the right side. A stabillo pencil is used to form a final line on the transfer paper, then cut it out in two steps, just like the other side.

The final step is to clearcoat the whole thing, a step that is done in a nearby make-shift paint booth.

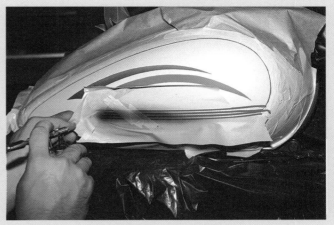

After masking out the lines with fine-line tape Bert creates the horizontal lines along the bottom.

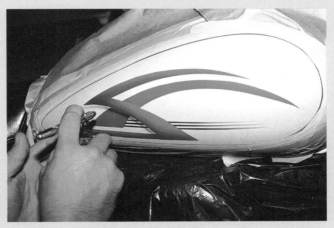

The depth comes from the shadows which make the spears float up above the surface.

The finished job, requiring no disassembly and only one afternoon without the motorcycle.

thanes are technically an enamel, they will be considered as a separate type of paint.

ENAMEL

Most modern enamels are acrylic enamels meaning they contain plastic for improved flexibility and durability. Enamel uses a reducer instead of a thinner, as the solvent part of the mix. An enamel paint job hardens as the reducer evaporates and the resin oxidizes (mixes with oxygen), meaning a longer drying time for an enamel paint job.

The long drying time means more time for dust to be trapped on the surface of the paint, and more time to wait to apply second coats or tape out a design.

LACQUER

Lacquer paints have been available for years and years. By the late 1950s everyone had switched to a new lacquer formula - acrylic lacquer. This new material used the acrylic to provide better resistance to ultraviolet radiation and also to give the paint more flexibility. The increased flexibility helped to eliminate most of the cracking that occurred with the earliest lacquers.

Custom painters have always liked lacquer because of it's fast drying times, low toxicity, great

color and the ease with which spot repairs can be made. These same characteristics make lacquers a favorite among back-yard painters working in less-than-ideal conditions. Custom painters often put lacquer on in multiple coats, wet sanding between coats. The end result is a deep shine that you can almost swim in and a perfectly smooth surface created by sanding between coats.

The trouble with acrylic lacquer is it's lack of durability (it chips and stains fairly easily) and the large amount of maintenance a lacquer paint job requires. The great lacquer shine comes only after plenty of wet sanding and polishing. Keeping the paint looking good means regular sessions with polish and wax. In the end, a good looking lacquer paint job requires a lot of maintenance.

The other problem with lacquer paints is the VOC issue discussed earlier. The evaporating thinner and the multiple coats (more thinner) means that spraying lacquer puts a relatively large amount of VOCs in the atmosphere. All this means lacquers are on their way out as a custom painting material.

URETHANE

The hot stuff in the custom painting field is urethane. Technically an enamel, urethane sprays much like a lacquer. Urethane is a two-part paint material catalyzed with isocyanate. Even though it's classed as an enamel, urethane dries very fast and offers easy spot repairs. The fast drying means quick application of second coats, easy candy paint jobs and fast tape outs for flame jobs and graphics. Unlike lacquer, urethane is super durable, resisting rock chips and chemical stains better than anything except powder coating.

Urethane can be used in a basecoat-clearcoat situation or as a one shot application. The biggest single downside to the urethane paints is the toxicity of the catalyst, the isocyanates. These materials are so toxic that spraying with urethanes requires a

It's a good idea to buy all the paint materials for a paint job from the same paint company so there are no problems with compatibility from one product to another. Bruce used materials from Xtreem, a relatively new company, for the big Honda.

fresh-air system (especially in the home painting "booth" where ventilation is limited) so the painter is sure to breathe absolutely no shop air. We need to mention the fact that many of the newer paint systems use urethane basecoats that are not catalyzed and thus don't require the elaborate safely precautions listed above. The other downside to urethanes is their higher cost.

CUSTOM PAINTS

Custom paint jobs are often applied in multiple layers. The first finish coat is called the basecoat. This base layer of paint can be any color or a metallic paint. The base coat can be covered by a candycoat or a clearcoat.

Candy colors were discovered in the 1950s when custom painters like Jon Kosmoski tried putting a little tint in a can of clear and then spraying the tinted clear over the base color. The final color in a candy paint job is a combination of the base color as seen through the tinted coat on top. The effect was much like looking through a piece of translucent colored candy. These new candy paint jobs became the hot ticket for both custom bikes and cars and remain so to this day. By combining different basecoats with different candy colors (and a different number of candycoats) an infinite number of colors are possible.

Most modern candy paint jobs contain three distinct layers of paint (some use only two coats). The basecoat, often a metallic or semi-metallic color, followed by the candy or tinted clear. Those two distinct layers are then topped by a clearcoat that guarantees a great shine and good resistance to ultraviolet rays. Sometimes the basecoat is a stand-alone color topped with a clearcoat for shine and protection. The multiple coats and distinct layers of paint give a good candy paint the depth that these paint jobs are known for.

Many of us are familiar with metallic paint jobs, tiny pieces that look like chopped tin foil are added to the paint by the manufacturer or the painter to provide extra sparkle. Metallics are currently available from a number of suppliers in both silver and gold finishes, and in a number of particle sizes.

Metallics add sparkle to a paint job, while pearls add a more subtle glow in much the same way. Some paints have the metallic particles already mixed with the paint, or you can buy raw particles in various sizes and mix them with the paint yourself. Pearl par-

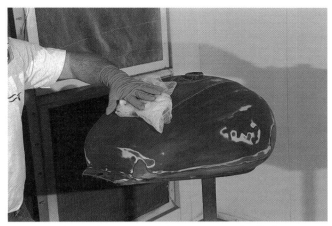

After applying the primer coats Bruce sands all the parts with 320 grit paper then wipes it down carefully with a tack rag.

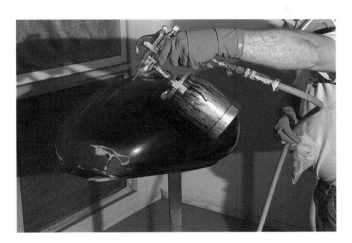

In order to ensure the tank is all one uniform color, Bruce applies a single coat of sealer before the actual painting begins.

This is the tank after application of two coats of bohemian black urethane. The black is then topcoated with two coats of inter-coat clear, which must be sanded with 600 grit paper before layout begins.

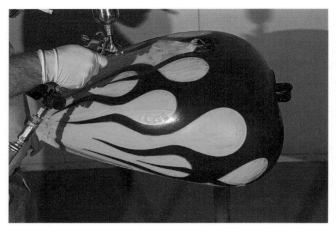

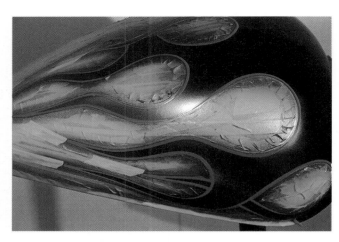

Bruce designs the flames with tape, right on the tank. Once the layout and masking are done the next step is two coats of silver (the pinstripe color) sprayed right next to the edge of the tape..

This is the tank after application of two coats of the blue near the ends of the flame licks.

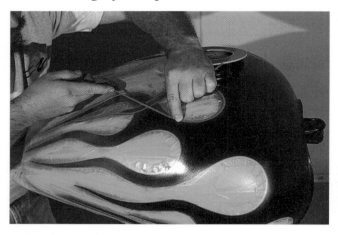

After drying the silver is covered with eighth inch fine-line tape from 3M. Now the rest of the painting can proceed. Later, when all the tape is pulled, the silver will be the pinstripe.

Application of the green basecoats, used about mid-lick, is next. Here you can see the flames after the second coat of green base. The next step is two coats of candy blue over the entire tank.

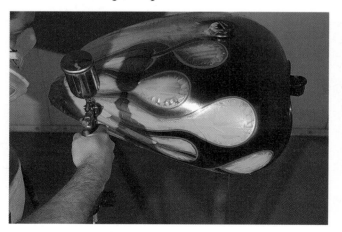

The flames will be multi-colored. The first step is to apply the blue basecoat paint to the flame ends.

As Bruce pulls the tape you can see how the taped over silver areas form a perfect pinstripe.

ticles are tiny bits of synthetic material added to the paint. The glow of a pearl job comes from the light that strikes the pearl flake and is then reflected to the viewer. The actual color you see depends on the color of the pearl particles, often acting in combination with the color of the basecoat or the tinted clearcoat.

The finished tank. The black areas are flat because they were sanded. The next step is multiple layers of clear, with sanding between coats to create a bright shine and a smooth surface.

Pearl paint jobs often react differently to different types and angles of light. Walking around a pearl job can be a little unsettling. From one direction you might see the blue base coat while from another you see the violet color reflected by the colored pearl chips (many painters describe this as flip-flop). A good pearl job has a lovely soft glow almost as though the light is shining through the paint from underneath.

Somewhat new on the paint scene are special "flip-flop" paints that change color very dramatically as you change the angle of viewing. Kameleon paint from House of Kolor changes color completely from one color to another depending on the type and angle of light.

Mild or wild, any paint you put on that motorcycle is guaranteed to have a major impact on the appearance. The cost may be high but the rewards are great as well. Visually, this is one of the most important things you're going to do to this bike. Take the time to consider carefully who does the work and exactly what they should do.

The finished bike owned by Evert Isaacson, complete with a Drag Specialties fairing and lady-bug bags from Corbin.

Chapter Eight

Styling Ideas

Spend Your Money Well

This chapter is intended to help you design that new (or re-newed) motorcycle. As we've said before, it's easy to throw parts at a bike. Despite the new gleaming parts and the sometimes large expenditure in cash, the results aren't always what the builder

intended. Worse, lots of money spent doesn't necessarily mean the end result is attractive or sexy or cool.

It is the intent of this book to help people build what might be called mild customs. Personalized

Hardly a radical bike, this Nomad uses a simple black paint job and just enough chrome accessories to create one very good looking motorcycle. Kawasaki

bikes with improved looks and performance, built on a budget.

To provide food for thought we've included an interview with Jeff Palhegyi, the man who designed and build a number of outstanding customs for Yamaha. In Chapter One there's another interview, this one with Arlen Ness.

What you're trying to do is personalize your machine. To ensure, as so many riders have explained to me, "That I'm not going to see a bike just like mine coming down the highway or in the parking lot at the rally."

What we've done is outline a few themes, as well as some ideas that are specific to certain models. You may not agree with our ideas, though they might make a good starting point for some better ideas of your own.

IT'S THE DESIGN STUPID

As already explained in Chapter One, the first and most important part of the project is planning. You need to know what you want the finished bike to look like before you start. For big projects you can hire an outside designer. For most of us, the logical plan is to collect photos of the bikes that turn us on. Based on a careful assessment of these photos you can decide what those bikes have in common and how the best of those design features can be included on our own machine.

The idea is to build a great looking bike without spending a million dollars.

A very nice Road Star. Note the classy two-tone paint, the billet headlight, extra chrome and nice wheels.

In Europe they build their cruisers with a strong performance flavor, almost like crossing a cruiser with a Ninja. Planet Cruiser

Another project bike, this one uses some very nice paint, a solo seat from Corbin, lowering kits from Progressive and a Vance and Hines Longshot exhaust system to create a very bright and desirable Drifter. Kawasaki

Some bikes just have the look. They sit exactly right and draw your eye away from anything else nearby. In order to achieve that certain allure and harmony in the way the bike looks you need to plan the bike. The paint, the accessories, the wheels and the stance are all part of what makes up the look of a certain machine. It's easier to get all those factors right with careful planning.

Before leaving this planning section it might be useful to consider the ways in which the bike can be "lowered" through the use of design and paint.

The concept is simple. Think about the Mustangs, Camaros and all the rest of the cars with their plastic "ground effects" molding and trim. The spoilers, extra deep bumper covers and wheel-arc trim all bring the bodywork closer to the ground, essentially "lowering" the car without actually changing any of the suspension members or dimensions.

The same thing can be done on two wheels by installing "tail-dragger" type fenders with tips that come close to the ground. To create the long and low impression, use long exhaust pipes that run the full length of the bike, and graphics of pinstripes made up of horizontal, rather than vertical, lines. A good example of this is the Victory with the scalloped paint job seen in the Dream Bikes section.

Remember that sometimes less is more. It's far too easy to add flames or graphics in yellow and purple, with

Like a beautiful model with exactly the right jewelry, this Nomad wears just enough chrome to complement the paint and create a certain elegance. Cobra

every chrome accessory in the factory catalog. The finished bike may be bright, but that doesn't mean it's good looking.

IDEAS

What follows are some dress-up ideas for a variety of bikes. Not all the models are represented here, we've chosen to focus on the most popular models from each manufacturer, though many of the ideas can easily be applied to similar models. If you don't like our ideas, that's fine, just substitute your own better ideas. The main goal is to make you think first and buy stuff second.

KAWASAKI

The Kawasaki Cruisers have achieved good acceptance on the street and the reasons are easy to understand. First, the 1500cc engine is one of the bigger V-twins in the class. Second, the bikes look good right off the floor. The 1500 comes in at least three separate models including the neo-Indian Drifter, the touring Nomad and the cruiser Vulcan.

Well received by both the press and the public, the Drifter line, also available in an 800cc model, has enormous potential as a custom. The big fenders and retro look give this bike an already customized look. In 2001 the big Drifter received a mild restyling. The newer bikes are brighter than those produced earlier and come with more chrome and brighter paint.

If your Drifter is a pre-2001 model one easy series of upgrades is simply to brighten the bike with chrome in place of the blacked out light housings, handle bars and dash. Next, replace the satin-finish engine covers and rocker box covers with some real chrome. Now go surfing through the Cobra or Kawasaki accessories catalog for just a few more plated accessories.

And then there's the matter of the two-up seat. That mass of black naugahyde and steel rails cantilevered over the

back fender kind of overwhelms the bike. Viewing the bike from the back it's all you see. The unusual seat is necessitated by the design of the rear suspension. Instead of moving the wheel and tire inside the fender, the fender moves with the wheel as the bike goes over bumps. Thus the seat must be positioned high enough up to clear the fender. Solo seats are available from Kawasaki, Cobra, and Corbin to mention only three. To say they change the looks of the bike is a major understatement. For an occasional passenger you could add a pillion, available from either the metric or Harley aftermarket, to the fender. In fact, temporary pillion pads are available with suction cups for instant installation and removal.

The only exception to the two-up-seats-are-ugly rule might be bikes with bags attached, as the bags help the seat to blend with the rest of the bike.

The Nomad, the touring model of the Kawasaki's cruising trinity starts life as a good looking touring rig, complete with stylish bags shaped to match the shape of the rear fender. Unlike the Vulcan with staggered mufflers on the right side, the Nomad comes to market with "duals," one muffler hanging below each bag. The relocated mufflers

Another example of good paint design combined with a few accessories and aftermarket exhaust. The effect is eye-catching without being neon-bright. Kawasaki

make more room for the bags but also gives the Nomad more bulk and the look of a classic dresser.

Customizing the Nomad is easy. It's a good looking bike to start with and the catalogs are filled with a multitude of accessories and exhaust systems for Kawasaki's touring cruiser. Before you start to bolt on extra lights and chrome rails to your wandering Kawasaki however, consider your overall plan for the bike.

Much of what's happening in the two-wheeled custom world might best be described as subtractive customizing. Instead of adding light bars and chrome trim, owners are removing the trim and crash bars. Turn signals, especially in the rear, are often replaced with smaller light housings mounted below the bags or between the bags and the fender. The really trick set up is to have LED lights flush-mounted into the backs of the bags themselves, though this is a lot of work and reduces the amount of gear you can stuff in the bag.

If you repaint your Nomad, consider painting the side cover/oil tank on the right side. On the stock bikes it always seems like a black hole, absorbing light right in the middle of the bike. If instead of a full paint job you opt to have some pinstripes or graphics added to the stock paint job, consider having the painter add something bright to the side cover.

HONDA

The Shadow series of bikes is a good case of creating a number of attractive models all based on either the 750 or 1100 cc mechanical platform. The Aero with it's art-deco styling cues is a great looking bike. Chrome side covers, complete with the ribs, are available from your local Honda dealer. And though we hesitate to recommend additional trim, Honda also makes a nice chrome front fender ornament that ties in nicely with the deco-look. You could even pull off the existing tank trim and have a good pinstripe artist add some horizontal lines to the tank, maybe even one or two long spears of gold-leaf. Remember that this design utilizes accents that run horizontally. The addition of vertical elements like sissy bars and higher handlebars run counter to the horizontal flow of these bikes.

Like the Aero, the A.C.E. comes to the showroom floor with nice lines and restrained chrome. Available in a touring model, many of these bikes are delivered in basic black. The basic paint job makes a great canvas for some tasteful pinstripes or graphics.

The Honda stylists didn't miss much when they penned this one. Note the trim front fender, the subtle arch to the tank, the bobbed rear fender with neo-Deuce taillight gobs of horsepower and good looks to boot. Honda

The bags in particular, with their flat outside surfaces, cry out for some painted accents.

Rear turn signal relocation kits are available from a number of sources. In the case of the touring model, oval lights can be tucked in between the bags and the fender. The Harley aftermarket makes filler-strips that mount between the bags and the fender so the bags become and extension of the fender. Clever builders often flush-mount the turn signals into these filler strips. there's no reason you couldn't have similar strips fabricated for your Honda and then add the lights.

Like other bikes in this section, Honda's Valkyrie is

available in a basic cruiser or a touring rig. What separates the Valkyrie from other cruisers is both the bulk and the brawn of a Goldwing on steroids. This is a cruiser that hauls ass. One very popular group of accessories play off the performance theme. Though the triple velocity stacks on each side are only for looks, they look so good that it doesn't matter. Working along that same theme, try discarding the stock six into two exhaust on each side, with a six into six system, available from your dealer and a number of firms in the aftermarket.

At this time the aftermarket doesn't have very many accessories for the big 1800cc Honda VTX. Never one to miss an opportunity, Honda did introduce their own line of accessories for the ultra-cruiser at the time the bike was introduced. The key here is the basic good looks of the bike. Anything you do should be designed to work within the styling parameters of the stock bike. And with trick flip-flop paint, it isn't likely that anyone will be in a hurry to repaint their VTX.

SUZUKI

The Intruder 1400 is one of the early Metric cruisers and it's still going strong. With the built-in forward controls, the low-down seating position and gas tank mounted on top of the frame the bike has the silhouette of a chopper from the 1970s. Changes to the bike could easily go in one of two directions. To enhance the chopper look you could add an even

Like the Nomad, the touring Hondas can be dressed to kill with extra trim, guards and light bars. Cobra

If you want to get rid of that big light bar on the back fender while retaining the OEM lights try this light relocation kit from Cobra.

An interesting design study. With only a few 'deco trim pieces and white side wall tires, Honda created a very successful new model. The little things do count.

The paint is bright, the accessories well chosen. Note the exhaust, the bullet tips on the fork and the velocity stacks (both from Aeromach), the solo seat and the flamed side cover.

smaller front fender (or no fender at all) along with taller ape-hanger handle bars and a side-mount license plate. You could also take the bike the other way with a gas tank that fits down over the frame (see the interesting Intruder in the Dream Bikes section), a set of flatter handle bars and a deleted sissy bar. The twin-shock rear suspension makes the bike an easy one to lower.

Suzuki's other big-inch cruiser, the Intruder 1500 suffers from a potential problem. Because the bike has never sold in huge volume, the number of available accessories is somewhat small. Yes, there are items in both the Cobra and the Suzuki catalog, but the selection is sparse. You can still rely on the old standards of paint, bars, pegs and lights. Discard the rear light bar and mount some smaller turn signals to the fenders. trade the stock pegs for something more to your liking from Küryakyn. Trade the stock bars for a set with built in risers.

VICTORY

Perhaps the best engineered cruiser ever brought to market, the Victory is not a bad looking motorcycle. Arlen Ness, America's best known designer, offers proof of the Victory's potential with the project bikes he's done for Polaris.

The stock, standard V92C looks a little stubby, though the problem can be

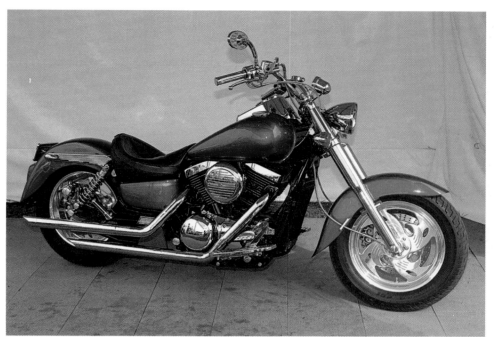

time on the design and engineering of these bikes so the customizing is easy. The bikes have nice metal fenders and hidden subframes under the rear fenders. Each one has a nice metal tank and many of those tanks have no lip around the bottom so it's in good shape to start with.

Here again, to me the most important thing is going to be custom paint and wheels. Wheels are going be expensive but there are some manufacturers that make billet wheels that will work with your existing

They don't have to be radical to be good looking, all you need is nice paint complemented by a certain amount of chrome and a good set of wheels.

remedied relatively easily with fresh paint and a few accessories. A sleek, one-piece seat from Corbin or Victory and a paint job with some horizontal lines help to stretch out the bike in a visual sense. If you want to get more involved, the huge rear light and turn-signal bar assembly cries out for something a little smaller, though that will probably involve work to the fender. There may not be as many aftermarket parts for the Victory as there are for some of the more popular metric models. With Arlen Ness on the job however, that situation is changing as we speak. The Victory accessory catalog includes all the standard chrome accents including chrome side covers, along with a range of Arlen's billet engine covers, grips, pegs, mirrors and all the rest.

For a look at what you can do to a Victory without changing the sheet metal consider the Dream Machine built by Ken Lee of Boiling Springs Cycle.

YAMAHA

For Yamaha customizing ideas we called the man who's modified more Yamahas than any other, Jeff Palhegyi. His comments follow:

First thing, if you are a Yamaha owner, you have made a good choice. If you bought one of the "Star" bikes, you have purchased something that was designed to be customized. Yamaha spent a lot of

If you're going to paint the bike anyway, why not change the look of the rear fender with a light assembly like this one from Arlen Ness.

Lights, Action

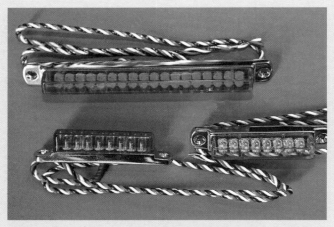

This is just a very small sample of the lights available at one store, Dr. Mudspringer in Minneapolis, MN.

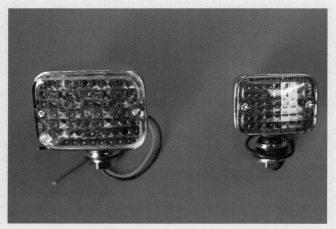

The relatively new LED lights offer bright light in a small package. 3 wires: low, bright and a ground.

Marker lights like these come in two sizes and are often used to replace the factory blinker lights.

CLEANING UP

Much of what we call customizing is really a matter of cleaning up the OEM design. In place of huge and often ugly light assemblies we install small svelte lights with billet housings. In the past five years the number of accessory lights designed specifically for the motorcycle market has simply exploded. Cobra, Arlen Ness, Küryakyn and all the big factories offer everything from traditional cat's eye taillights to new LED and halogen designs. If you can't find what you want in the local dealership take a stroll through the local aftermarket shop, both the metric and the V-twin store offer hundreds of designs.

You can have tapered assemblies designed to blend in when bolted to a rear fender strut, or trim accessory lights with integral brackets that easily mount to the fork tubes. If what you're trying to do is keep the turn signals but somehow make them less obtrusive, Arlen Ness offers lights that mount to the stem of his mirrors. Or you can mount the turn signals at the ends of the handle bars with assemblies from Planet Cruiser and others.

There are a couple of things to keep in mind when replacing the factory lights with something better. A number of accidents occur because the auto drive simply didn't "see" the bike. When replacing the factory lights try to place them on the bike where they do the most good, and don't go to extreme lengths to minimize the size of the light because then you minimize its light output as well. At least ensure the brake and taillight you use is as bright as the stock light. Extra bright halogen bulbs, which replace the standard, two-contact 1157 bulb, are available for those light assemblies that just don't throw as much light as a stock unit does.

The aftermarket LED lights are a good alternative here as they manage to be very cool and quite bright at the same time. The small "bullet" lights are another good choice as the amount of

Lights, Action

light that comes out of these is simply astounding.

The other thing you need to consider when buying and replacing lights is the DOT. Many of the lights you lust after are not "DOT approved." You probably don't give a damn, unless you happen to live in a state with tough inspection laws, or you get pulled over by an overzealous high patrol officer some night. Speaking of lights and legality, the traditional "blue dot" lights, used for years on custom cars, always look to me like a good way to meet a lot of really nice police officers.

BOLT THEM ON RIGHT

Bolting the new lights to the bike might be more work than you think. Wiring is the one place where even pretty good mechanics seem to slide into slip-shod work. So try to keep the following in mind when installing those trick new lights from Arlen or Cobra or Highway Hawk.

First, be neat. Route the wires carefully so they don't rub on a tire or get pinched between the bracket and the frame. Professional custom builders often put the wires inside the bars or the frame. You may not want to go to those lengths, but at least use some tie wraps (available in numerous colors and sizes) to keep the wires out of harm's way. Protect exposed or vulnerable wires with grommets or a larger piece of tubing.

Second, make a good electrical connection. Solder the connections and use shrink-wrap on the connection to insulate and protect the joint. Avoid using crimp-connectors, especially in places where there's likely to be plenty of moisture, like under the fenders. If the light has no separate ground wire it must have a good connection to the frame in order to operate. Sometimes a star washer used between the light-body and the fender or frame can help provide that connection to the bike's ground.

Available in two sized, these silver bullets use a halogen bulb and are very BRIGHT. Küryakyn

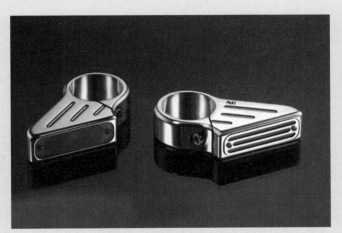

Clamp these billet accessory lights to the fork tubes and eliminate those ugly factory lights. Planet Cruiser

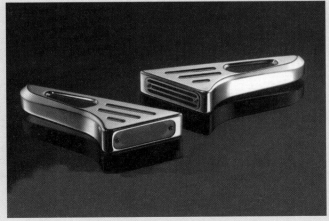

At the back of the bike you can bolt these slim sexy units to the fender rail. Planet Cruiser

brakes. Performance Machine and RC Components are two companies that I use. Both companies manufacture wheels for the Road Stars that allow you to use their wheel and hub with the stock brake calipers and rotors. This alone will save you over 50% of the cost versus changing all that out and putting on billet rotors and calipers. This is one way you can put larger diameter wheels or sportier looking tires on the bike and keep your budget low. With paint too, you can go with a stan-

Built by Suzuki to show what can be done with the big Intruder, this machine utilizes many Suzuki accessories and a very trick paint job.

Most big paint companies utilize some form of the color change paint. These paints use pigments that change color depending on the angle of the light.

dard base coat paint not a three-stage paint. It's less expensive to shoot, with the painters I use the cost is somewhere around a third less because its not a three-stage paint. There are plenty of colors that go well together. You can have a real nice look and save some money too.

INTERVIEW WITH JEFF PALHEGYI

One of the best known customizers working in the metric market is Jeff Palhegyi. In the interview that follows Jeff shares some of his philosophies and design ideas.

Jeff, can we start with some background. How did you get into customizing motorcycles?

When I started working for Yamaha in 1989 I did primarily ATV design and development. I built prototypes and concept vehicles for Yamaha. With the introduction of the Royal Star in 1996 I saw the opportunity to do something different and I knew about the dealer introduction coming up so I asked Yamaha if I could have one to customize. It was called Cookies 'n Cream and it was a 1996 Yamaha Royal Star custom. Tom Taylor was the painter, it was my very first custom motorcycle. I tried to take the elements that Yamaha had given us with the Royal Star and accentuate them via longer fenders, different wheels, custom paint and chrome plating. I was trying to maintain a classical image as the Royal Star is a retro-styled bike.

Can you describe the process you go through in designing and building one of the bikes you've done for Yamaha. Do you do an elaborate drawing of the bike or do you work without drawings?

When we build a custom bike for Yamaha there is usually some sort of initial idea. We might have a brain-storming session at one of the rallies like Sturgis or Daytona. We always try to build something that customers themselves would be able to relate to. Some of the things that we do customers themselves can do, mostly custom paint, accessories and custom wheels.

Sometimes on a real elaborate bike like the blue wish, we have to make drawings to nail down the concept and make sure it's going to flow together. Anytime we're doing elaborate body modifications we will make some sketches and layouts just to make sure everything is going to work. If we are chopping the frame for instance and planning to use long stretched fenders we do a layout on paper to check clearances and shapes to make sure we're going to end up with the desired look. We try not to build bikes that look the same. We might build one that has a short rear fender and one that has a long rear fender. We may end up building two of each bike because there are two different motorcycle tours that travel across the country.

With a fat bob rear fender and nice lines, the Suzuki Marauder makes a good looking bike. Add a new seat and a little more chrome to make this a killer cruiser built on a budget.

The engine is very much a part of the bike's visual package. For this Yamaha display bike they dressed the big V-twin in abundant chrome and painted the rest of the engine to match the bike.

For the most part though we try to skip around and get some different looks. Maybe a drag look or a pro-street classic style look, maybe something simple.

Where do you get most of your ideas or concepts?

I either have something in my mind that I want to build or I've seen something at a rally that looks like it will work with the Road Star or the V-Star and I say 'hey! I can do that with our bike and I think people are going to get excited about seeing that in the Yamaha product.' We see a lot of stuff at rallies and sometimes you come up with a totally new idea like the Sumo. Sumo is a Road Star that we built with 10 inch wide tires. Somebody at Yamaha said, 'hey can you do that?' and I said sure! Therefore, the ideas come from everywhere.

Can you discuss some of your design goals in terms of shapes and how you ensure that the design flows from one end to the other? That all the parts work together in a visual sense?

The main thing is to have an idea and a theme from the very beginning. What is the bike going to be? If it is a classic style bike you probably want to use spoked wheels. You should try to have some continuity with all of your parts. You do not typically build a classic style bike with billet bike wheels, for example.

You have to match everything up, match your accessories and your body work. I go to all of the events and a lot of times a guy will have a Harley-Davidson with a stock rear fender and he'll use an aftermarket front fender that doesn't work with the rear fender. When you're looking at a really good design you're going to see that everything flows together. The tank lines, the lines on the fenders, the side covers, any of the body components typically will be styled to match.

This is also true of the accessories theme, it will be carried out from front to rear. You either have a smooth clean look, a framed look, a ball-milled look or just a simple bare-necessities look. There are a lot of different ways to go. But, the main thing to keep in mind so it all works together in a visual sense - everything has got to match. There's got to be continuity in your design, you've got to have a plan from the very beginning and follow it through. Sometimes it takes a lot of work in checking around to find all the right pieces to make that happen but its worth while and it shows in the end product.

How about mistakes. When people build a bike that doesn't work, that just doesn't look good, where are the mistakes?

Some of the mistakes people make will be with mismatched accessories and paint. I have seen many, many beautiful bikes just botched with paint. Sometimes they have a really clean look, really smooth bodywork and they put too much obscene paint all over it. They spend so much money on paint and so often its not the kind of look that's appealing to people, its real busy and complex. There again if you're going after that custom look you want a paint job that's going to accentuate the look of the bike.

Another well appointed Road Star with elaborate 3-D paint, a custom seat and abundant bright work.

For people working at home on less elaborate projects, should they take the time to do a drawing or a sketch of the "new" bike.

The main thing for people to do at home is to get the look of their bike figured out from the very beginning. Maybe they can cut out magazine pictures and then think about colors and look at accessories. It helps to take photos of bikes and things you like. Lay it all out on a table and if you have good drawing skills you can make a concept drawing. The best thing to do is to get everything photographed and in your mind, lay it all out before you start. You might have the bike all ready, but try to get your ideas all laid out so everything goes together.

Can you talk about the importance of paint, especially for individuals who aren't building a full-on custom?

Paint is huge! I've seen stock bikes with the right paint job look incredible. And a lot of times its not even how wild the paint job is, but how much time was taken in selecting colors that would be different but work well together, achieving that special look. A lot of times people just paint the bikes all black. In the cruiser market place black bikes seem to be pretty popular and it looks great but everyone has that same look. You need to know your painter, have some samples of his or her work.

If you're not sure about paint or paint designs take some photos, look at cars,

Two customs from Victory, one a very bare-bones bar-hopper, the other a full dresser.

Deep Purple is the first Road Star built by Jeff Palhegyi. Like many of his bikes it uses long fenders and a stretched tank to create some very pleasing lines. Dave Bush

brand new model cars. Look at what is popular and what colors go well together. Go to an autobody supply shop and get a paint chart, cut the color chips out, put them next to each other, hold them up in the sun and get an idea of what they're going to look like.

You might want to bring sketches, or photos of something that's similar to your idea, to the painter. That way your painter has a full understanding of what you want in the finished product.

Assuming they're not doing

Jeff built Tequila simply to show how cool they could make a small shaft-drive motorcycle. Dave Bush

Tequila uses factory wire wheels combined with an aftermarket rotor up front. Front and rear wheels are wrapped by long swoopy aftermarket fenders. Dave Bush

a full-custom, do you have ideas as to how they might create a nice-looking, personalized bike while using the stock sheet metal and staying within a reasonable budget.

I have seen many nice bikes that were done on a budget. For your custom look, a paint job can achieve a radically different look. A lot of times you'll see really nice customized bikes that are entry level bikes, like our V-Star 650. People have a $6,000 dollar bike and they do not want to spend another $6,000 dollars customizing it. They have done things simple like blackout some of the pieces that are on the bike, add some custom paint and small chrome pieces. Chroming is not that expensive and it's a good way to achieve a personalized look. Stock sheet metal in most cases can look very nice with custom paint, which again is kind of the key to the overall look of a custom bike.

In conclusion I would like to say if you're building a custom bike, specifically a metric cruiser, you need to look around at what the manufacturers are showing. What Yamaha and Kawasaki are doing with their customs is important, because they have access to all of the aftermarket parts. Their show bikes and calendar bikes are going to give you a good concept of what is available and how far you can go with your ideas.

Yamaha has a large after-market accessory display that they show at some of the big rallies. It's a good idea to look at what is available before you start. It was extremely difficult in the beginning to customize a metric bike because nobody made the components, but now it is unlimited as to what you can achieve.

Do not sell yourself short. Figure out a total budget and how much you're willing to spend in the next couple of years. Plan a sequence of events and follow that plan to accomplish your goals.

During the evolution of Blue Wish, seen below, Jeff tried a pair of Mikuni carburetors – which gives the bike much more of a go-fast attitude.

Blue Wish is one of Jeff's personal machines. He describes the bike as, "An extreme custom, with the emphasis on the large motor and wheels and minimalist body work." Dave Bush

Chapter Nine

Accents and Accessories

Less May be More

Though some of the parts in this chapter qualify as trinkets, others are too important to ignore. While you can overdo the chrome accessory thing, it's hard to build a good looking bike without just the right combination of bolt-on goodies. Call them accents, or replacements for the ugly stuff they bolted on at the factory. They are an essential part of a nice personalized motorcycle.

We've broken the chapter down into logical sections. Handler bars, pegs, seats and all the rest. The

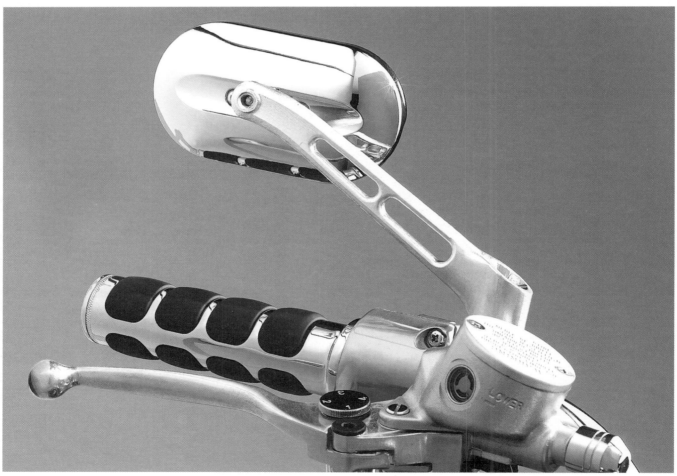

The Küryakyn designers seem to specialize in simple classic shapes that work, like this oval mirror and iso-grips

illustrations provide a look at what other riders are doing with their machines.

HANDLE BARS

Another of those topics that seems at first to be too simple, handle bars include not only the bars, but the grips, mirrors and controls at either end. And we haven't talked about the risers or the cables yet. From the good-news department comes the fact that nearly all the current crop of cruisers use handle bars that are one inch in diameter. Unlike the smaller bars used on some sport bikes and earlier cruisers, the one inch diameter is the same size as that used by Harley-Davidson. This means that not only are there a large number of offerings from the metric market, but that bars, risers and grips from the huge American V-Twin aftermarket can be used as well.

Both comfort and style are at stake here. The handle bars are probably the second thing that most riders change, right after they put on their first custom exhaust system. And though there may be only four bolts holding those bars in place, there's more here than meets the eye.

Like all the other parts of the bike, the bars should "go with the flow." Ape hanger bars don't belong on a café-style bike but they're an integral part of a chopper. A bike with a ultra fat rear tire and a high performance theme probably needs a pair of drag bars. So the bars you pick need to match the style of the bike. If it's a low slung bike you probably want to stay with some low profile bars.

Hardly your standard grips. This multitude of knurled and curled aluminum is more of the Euro-look from Planet Cruiser.

The bars, grips and mirrors are important for both comfort and looks. These wide beach bars and billet clamp come from the Cobra catalog.

Width is partly a matter of style and partly a matter of function. Big fat cruiser bikes look good with boulevard bars as wide as the horns on a Texas long-horn.

Before buying bars consider the practical stuff first. The bars must clear the tank when the fork is turned full lock in either direction. By clearance we mean at least the width of a finder between the upper triple trees or the bars, and the gas tank. At the grips themselves you obviously need more clearance than the width of your finger. What seems like enough clearance in the shop may not be enough when you're out in the real world. What happens, for example, if you bump the curb while idling up into a parking place. Or worse, drop the bike, even gently, in the parking lot. The additional force of even a minor spill can move the grips just a little past "full lock." It's bad enough you have to replace the lever and maybe have some paint work done, you don't want to pay the painter to take the big dent out of the tank at the same time.

The other issue that crops up when you change bars is the length of the cables and hydraulic lines. If the new bars and risers effectively move the outer ends of the bars very far back or to the sides you may have to replace the cables and lines. In cases like this the temptation may arise to re-route the cables and this gain a little length.

Consider though that the factory probably spent a lot of time determining the best position for those cables and lines. If you stretch the line to the master cylinder on the right side you could end up rupturing the brake line. A too-tight throttle cable can open the throttle when the bars are turned all the way over, giving you a boost of speed when you least need it.

New, longer, cables and lines are available from all the major suppliers, though their installation will add to the cost and complexity of your little project. If you're buying new cables anyway, consider those with a stainless braided outer housing, especially if you've replaced the front brake hoses and some of the oil lines with braided hose.

In most cases the bars connect to the bike through a set of "risers," the connection between the upper triple tree and the bars themselves. Though there are some bars out there with integral risers, most still use a separate connection to the triple clamp. When buying bars and risers the first requirement should be comfort and the ease with which you control the bike. If you like your bars but want more of a laid-back riding position, you can always use a taller riser or one that sweeps back, to move the bars closer to your body.

When it comes to looking for risers, that old phrase "if you can't find the ones you want you aren't looking hard enough" comes to mind. The catalogs from Planet Cruiser, Cobra, Küryakyn, Parts Unlimited and all the rest contain page after page of risers in steel and aluminum. Everything from very traditional designs that could have been lifted off an old Harley to the most modern sweeping shapes cut from billet aluminum.

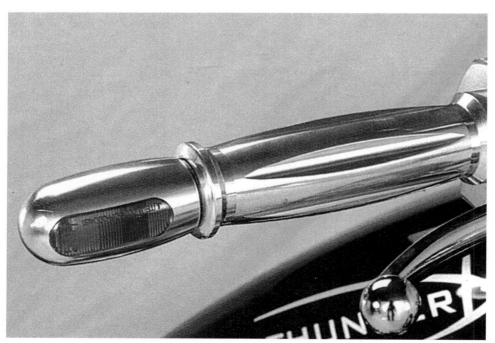

You can get the big blinker lights off the bike and give a whole new Euro-look with these bar-end lights and billet grips form Planet Cruiser.

GRIPS, CONTROLS AND MIRRORS

At the end of the bars are the grips, an integral part of your motorcycle's design. Again, there's everything here from the simple and traditional black foam grips to billet shapes cut to resemble something from the Space Shuttle. Two points need to be made here. First, most of the big aftermarket companies offer a complete line of grips, accessories and pegs with the same essential design. One of the best examples is Küryakyn with their Iso-pegs or Arlen Ness with their flamed or billet designs. By using the same design for the grips and the pegs you achieve a nice harmony in the bike's design. The second point involves your comfort. Some of the fluted billet designs we've tried look really cool, but the edges carved into the shape make it uncomfortable to hold onto the grip for more than ten minutes at a time. Try to buy something with the design you like and enough concessions to comfort that you aren't forced to wear leather gloves in order to ride the bike in July.

Closely related to the topic of grips is the subject of levers and controls. Assuming most people in this market are going to retain the stock controls and master cylinder(s), they (you) still have the option of adding levers, mirrors and new covers.

New levers include nearly-stock designs with a wider area where your fingers wrap, designed to ease finger fatigue in traffic, or sexy ribbed and

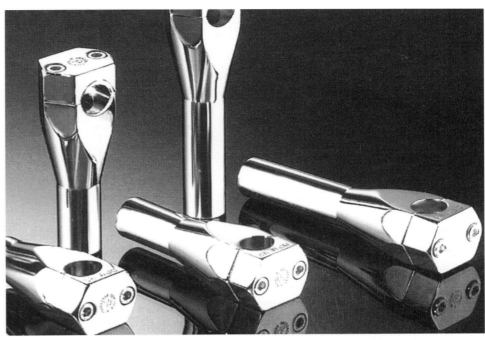

How you attach the bars to the bike is almost as important as the bars themselves. These unique risers come in lengths that range from stubby to tall. Planet Cruiser

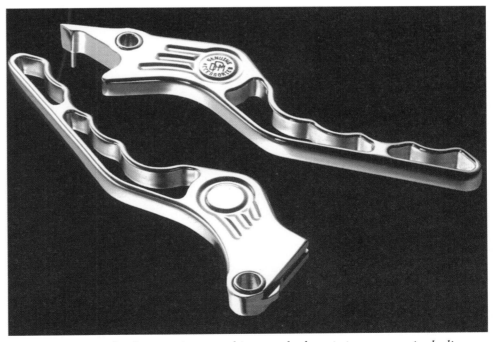

Once you get right down to it, everything on the bars is important, including the levers and controls. The cast aluminum designs are from Planet Cruiser

Said to be the "perfect blend of style and comfort," these Iso-Grips come with a small colored ring or accent at the end. Küryakyn

pistol-grip designs. If you have to change the levers, you need to find that same compromise between form and function.

Most mirrors screw into a boss that's part of the control assembly. Before buying mirrors you have to decide if you really want to see what's going on behind you. Because the trickest mirrors are often so small or use such a convoluted shape you'll never see much more than your own shoulder or a blur of Pontiacs and Peterbuilts.

Being mostly from overseas the cruisers in this market use metric threads on the base of the mirrors. Which makes it hard to use any designs from the American V-Twin aftermarket. Küryakyn (and probably others) make adapters that are American threads on one end and metric on the other to facilitate the use of "American" mirrors in a control assembly tapped with metric threads. Of course there are a vast number of aftermarket mirrors designed specifically for the metric market as well.

When buying bars, grips, and mirrors in particular, think about how they relate to the rest of the bike. Try to pick a mirror or grip design that's similar to the designs or shapes used throughout the rest of the bike. Before buying angular or square mirrors think about your motorcycle, a design dominated by two very large and very round objects, the wheels and tires. The same philosophy applies to the shape of the headlight and headlight nacelle.

By purchasing accessories in sets from the same company the bike takes on a more finished appearance. These Iso-Wings are meant to match the design of the grips. Küryakyn

PEGS, FLOORBOARDS AND FORWARD CONTROLS

After looking at the cast and polished floorboards or the carefully carved billet pegs available from the aftermarket the stock stamped floorboards or rubber-wrapped OEM pegs start to look pretty inadequate. Floorboard designs run the gamut from stamped steel to billet aluminum. From overseas come elaborate designs with deep cast fins and ribs.

Replacing the stock pegs or floorboards with something with more style and quality from the aftermarket is a pretty safe bet. Moving the controls from a typical stock position, where the peg or board is roughly below your butt, to a forward control is a much bigger deal. Before making the move to forward controls try riding a bike that's so equipped to ensure you actually like the position.

Installing forward controls is much more work and money than simply swapping pegs. On the left side there's the control itself to mount and the shift linkage to connect. On the right side the stock master cylinder generally goes away only to be replaced with the new master cylinder that's part of the forward control assembly. Some forward control assemblies off a much wider range of adjustments, making it easier to tailor the position of the peg itself to better suit your size ten boot.

Though style often takes a front seat to comfort, the pegs or floorboards should be mounted in a position that you, and only you, find comfortable.

These heavy duty floorboards are cast rather than carved from billet, and come with a matching heel-and-toe shifter. Planet Cruiser

Classic elegance on the end of the bars. A chrome plated swirled grip, with a new-look lever. Arlen Ness

Ten Minutes or Less

These billet running boards (part number K-1031) are a direct replacement for the boring black boards that come on many of the Kawasakis.

Two 6mm bolts (10mm heads) hold each running board in place. Wayne is seen here installing the new board with the bolts that come up from underneath. Yes, Wayne recommends putting Loctite on the bolts.

During a recent visit with Cory Ness he explained that they had a number of new products for the Kawasaki Vulcan, all of them designed as simple, bolt-on pieces. "In fact," promised Cory, "I don't think any of them take more than ten minutes to install". Before we could say "prove it," Cory had Wayne installing each piece on the resident Kawasaki Vulcan while the clock and the motor-drive clicked away. The end result documents the easy installation of some very nice accessories for the Vulcan, though most would fit the Nomad and Drifter as well

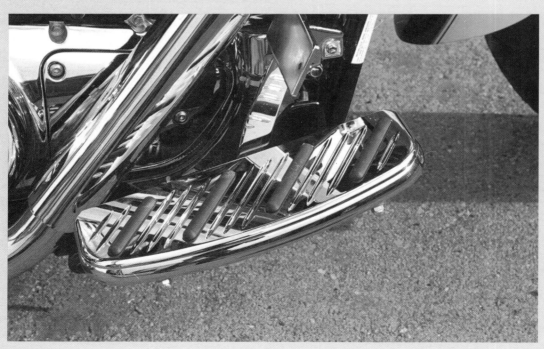

The finished project. A very quick way to add some glitter and class to that big Kawi. A matching brake lever cover is aslo available.

Ten Minutes or Less

This master cylinder cover, (#K-1015) is a very simple piece to install. A quick way to add some nice chrome detail to the bars.

It doesn't get much easier than this billet strip for the gas tank. Because it's a glue-on piece, Wayne recommends cleaning the tank thoroughly before you peel the covers off the strips seen here.

You have to know exactly where you want the cover to go - before sticking it down.

Ten Minutes or Less

A nice chrome gas cap cover (#K-1004) can be installed in five minutes. The cap is held on by the three screws seen here (maybe put a rag over that open hole so the screw doesn't go down inside the tank).

The results are bright and nearly instantaneous. The billet dash insert seen in the background is a prototype part number K-1010. The finished inserts will include the three lights.

Many of the available after-market mirrors require some kind of adapter between the boss on the controls and the mirror itself.

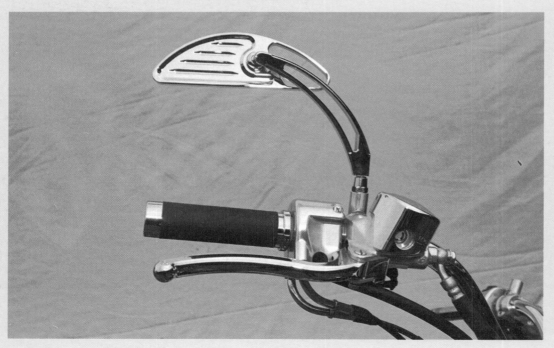

With the adapter in place it's a simple matter to install a pair of billet mirrors from the Arlen Ness catalog.

Ten Minutes or Less

To install the fender rail cover (#K1019) Wayne unscrews the two end screws on each fender rail and installs a collar under each one.

A lot of riders are replacing the levers. Removal of the OEM units means first taking off the nut on the bottom...

Once the two collars are in place on the two end bolts, as seen here, the cover can be slipped into place.

... the next step is to unscrew the small bolt shown here.

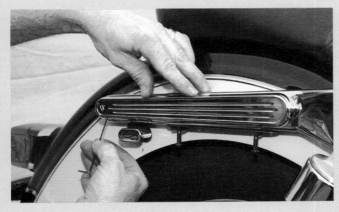

The final step is to tighten the set screws that lock the fender rail cover in place.

The replacement levers (#K-1013) make a nice compliment to the master cylinder cover.

Replacing the calipers, or sending them out to be plated, is a big, expensive, job. Far easier to simply attach covers like these from Cobra.

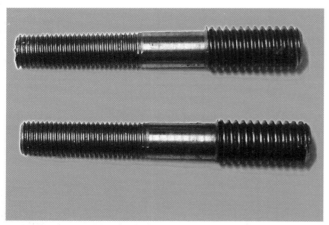

These riser studs allow the use of Harley-type risers on Kawasakis. Thunder Mfg.

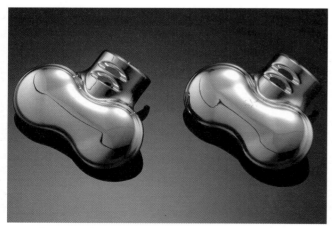

Another set of chrome plated caliper covers, this time for Kawasaki Vulcans. Require no tools for installation. Küryakyn

CARE OF THE FANNY

People who don't ride motorcycles, or don't take the time to personalize their own machines, only see the seat as someplace to rest their fanny while going down the road. The rest of us see the seat as an integral part of the machine, as much a part of the styling as the paint job or the accessories.

Think about the position of the seat. Not the obvious fact that it's in the middle of the bike, but the less obvious fact that it "connects" the gas tank with the rear fender. Recent seat designs that merge the seat with the tank at the front end, and taper to nothing on top of the fender, reflect this fact.

In a styling sense the seat can either make a stumpy bike look sleek or a sleek bike look stumpy. If you're trying to get the bike's lines to flow smoothly from front to back you don't want a huge seat with a raised "queen" section positioned on top of the fender. Sissy bars and backrests have a similar effect on the bike's looks. If you want a sissy bar or a seat with a back rest, then go for it. In some cases, like a chopper theme, the sissy bar might be just the thing. Like all the other parts of the bike you need to spend time thinking about the affect the seat has on the bike's design.

Some aftermarket seats mount using the factory mounting points. Others require that you drill some new holes or find your own way to attach the seat. This isn't rocket science but there are a few points that should be made. First, If you use a bolt or screw to hold the back of the seat in place, BE SURE THAT BOLT CAN'T TOUCH THE TIRE WHEN THE SUSPENSION BOTTOMS. We mentioned in the fenders section the need for any hardware used under the fender to point up and away from the tire, and the obvious advantage of using button-head bolts so that if the tire does touch the head of the bolt on a bump it won't rip the rubber off the tire.

Remember that you do need access to the battery or tools or oil tank hiding under the seat. The means you use to attach the seat must allow for quick access.

Some of the custom builders use hook-and-loop fasteners for all or part of their seat-mounting system. This allows instant access and no holes in the fender. Custom Chrome makes a nifty little stud and pin affair for the rear mount on the seat. The three piece design includes a tapped fixture that is located to the fender with a machine screw that comes up from under the fender. Once mounted it leaves a small stud sticking up out of the fender. The seat's mounting tab is lowered over the stud and a pin is inserted in to the hole in the stud. A small detent holds the pin in place. To take off the seat you only have to slip the pin out of place and lift off the seat.

NUTS, BOLTS AND COVERS

The nuts and bolts that hold your machine together can also be a big part of the details that separate a so-so bike from a really nice one. High quality fasteners are covered elsewhere in a side bar. The topic here is the wide range of covers available for either "Allen" bolts or hex-headed nuts. In the case of the socket headed cap-screws, you can snap a small chrome cover into the female socket and thus add a smooth shine to the fastener and also cover any rust that may have developed down inside the socket.

Chrome, snap-on covers can also be purchased for common 10, 12 and 14mm bolt heads. Covers for bigger nuts, like those used on the end of the axles, are also available from a variety of sources.

Additional, specific covers and chrome accessories could fill a book of their own. A few worth noting include chrome covers for the drive-shaft tubes on most shaft-driven cruisers. Also available for most cruisers are the bullet-shaped caps for the end of the

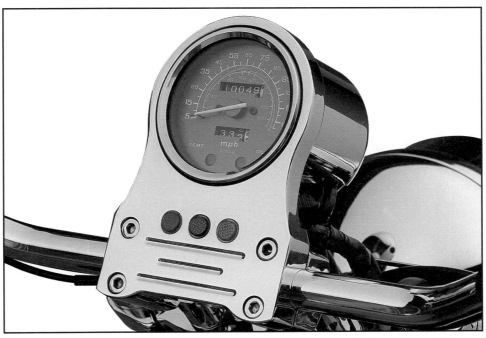

Clean up the bars with this speedometer and chrome billet housing complete with warning lights. Cobra

Not your average forward controls, this set features very high quality parts and lighted foot pegs. Planet Cruiser

A simple solo seat tends to simplify the bike and give it a more business like attitude. Many are available with or without a pillion pad. Cobra

Seats like these tend to enhance the bike's lines and make it look longer and lower. Unlike the "saddle" type seat these also allow the rider to move around a bit while on the road. Cobra

fork tubes. Already mentioned are the covers available for most brake calipers. The list here is long but a variety of hub caps are available for stock wheels and hubs. Even Yamaha sells billet-look covers that attach to the inside of the front wheel rotors on many of their bikes.

CHROME OR POLISHED?

Many of the larger accessories available for your cruiser come in either chrome or a polished finish. Many of the aluminum wheels, for example, come in either a polished or a plated version. If you get seriously bitten by the customizing bug, you may also begin to pull some parts off and send them out to the polishing or chrome plating shop. At first the two finishes may look nearly identical. Certainly the shine of a freshly polished cover like that seen in Chapter One is nearly as bright as the sheen seen on a similar chrome cover. If chrome costs more and the two finishes are similar, why not save some money and go with the polished surfaces whenever possible?

Two points should be made. First, even with a freshly polished cover the two finishes are different. It depends on who did the polishing, but polished aluminum has a softer look that some people actually prefer. The trouble comes six months or a year later when the aluminum has started to oxidize. Now there is no contest. The chrome is still shiny while the polished aluminum is starting to dull noticeably. Point number two: Yes, you can bring it back to the original shine with some Mothers or Semi-chrome polish, but that's the whole point.

Riders who've owned more than one custom seem to prefer to spend their time riding. Maintaining a nice bike and keeping it clean is a lot of work. They don't want the extra work of rubbing down wheels and covers two or four times per season or before each show. They advise spending the extra money for chrome plated parts and accessories.

There is one more thing to be considered here. Some would call it a case of being overly anal. The point is this: Chrome and polish do have different surfaces, especially if the polishing isn't fresh. Try to stick with one or the other for the whole machine. At least avoid the tendency to bolt a polished caliper to a chrome plated fork leg, where the contrast in the two surfaces is most apparent.

Whether your bike uses chrome or polished parts, we all like a little extra shine and in most cases the brightness improves the overall looks of the bike. There is a case, however, for restraint. Too many trinkets distract the viewer from really seeing the bike hidden underneath. So like all the other things most of us really like, you have to use a bit of moderation in the amount of chrome or billet you bolt onto that two-wheeled steed.

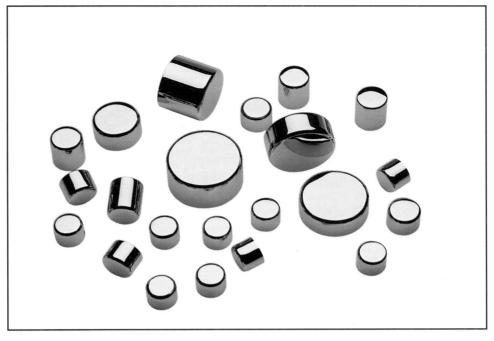

You can cover almost any of those unsightly nuts with nice chrome covers like these. Cobra

Though they don't do anything for the fork's function, these bullets certainly help out in the looks department. Available for most current cruisers from Aeromach.

Chapter Ten

Fasteners

Holding it all Together

Fasteners, what we often call nuts and bolts, are the devices that hold our bikes together. When you upgrade from the factory bolts to high quality "Allen" bolts, you've improved the machine in both a functional and an aesthetic sense. As Laura Brengelman from *Motorcycle Tour & Cruiser* magazine explained, "A lot of people don't realize that you can add detail with better bolts."

This is a short introduction to the topic of fasteners, a topic about which many weighty volumes have

They're more than just nuts 'n bolts, the fasteners and hardware define the machine. Use cheap "junk" bolts from the hardware store only if the bike is a cheap junky motorcycle.

been written. Much of this material is extracted from another Wolfgang book: *Hot Rod Hardware.*

WHAT'S A CAPSCREW

A bolt is nothing more than a threaded fastener designed to screw into a hole or nut with matching female threads. Technically a bolt is a fastener without a washer face under the head, while a capscrew has a washer face under the head. All metric "bolts" have a washer surface under the head and thus are capscrews.

AMERICAN THREADS

What American mechanics often call NC and NF or national course and national fine, are actually UNC and UNF. Or unified national course and unified national fine. This system came out of the confusion that arose during WWII when English mechanics tried to repair American Airplanes with Whitworth nuts and bolts. The "unified" system the allies settled on retained most of the then-current American standards and specifications.

Most shade-tree mechanics are familiar with SAE graded fasteners. These carry the radial dashes on the head that indicate their strength. No dashes is a cheap hardware store bolt. Three dashes is a Grade 5 while six identify the bolt as a Grade 8.

All bolts are measured in pounds per square inch of tension or stress. The ultimate tensile strength or UTS is the point at which the bolt breaks. The other specification given for quality bolts is the yield point, the point at which the bolt is stretched so far it will no longer bounce back to its original dimension once the stress is removed.

THE METRIC SYSTEM

In the metric system thread pitch is expresses as the distance in millimeters from one crest to the next, instead of as the number of threads per some unit of measurement. Common pitch specifications include

A good capscrew has a raised bearing surface just under the head. The nylon-collar type lock-nut shown is generally considered more effective than a split-ring lock washer.

Three random bolts. Left to right, a Grade 5, a 8.8 Metric bolt – roughly equivalent to a Grade 5 - and a Grade 8. Note that all have the manufacturer's headmark.

1.0, 1.25 and 1.50 mm. One of the problems with the metric system is the fact that there are four slightly different metric "systems" though the ISO (International Standards Organization) specifications seem to be dominant. This is why a 8 mm bolt used on your bike might have a 12 mm head while the one you get at the bolt supply house has a 13mm head. An 8 mm bolt will commonly be available in 1.0 and 1.25 mm thread pitch.

The grade of a metric bolt or capscrew is indicated with a two or three-digit number found on the head. Three of the most common gradings are 8.8, 9.8 and 10.9. Though the ratings are given in Newtons per square millimeter they can be converted to the SAE grading many of us are familiar with as follows. An 8.8 is roughly equivalent to a SAE Grade 5 with a rating of 120,000 psi for UTS, while a 10.9 is roughly the same as a SAE Grade 8 with an UTS of 150,000 psi.

A LITTLE HEAD

Socket Headed Cap Screws are the preferred fastener for many custom bike builders. Industrial "Allen" bolts, whether Unified or metric, are very strong. Both

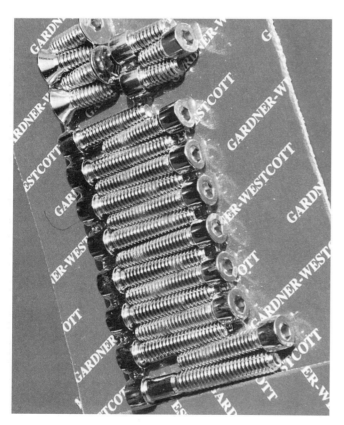

Gardner-Wescott makes a variety of decorative kits designed to fit one particular application.

carry ratings of at least 170,000 psi for ultimate tensile strength (better than a SAE Grade 8). Chrome and stainless SHCS don't necessarily meet these same standards.

The small head, which many see as an advantage, can be a problem, however. The small size means it's hard to use the full strength of the bolt to clamp things together. And if you use a standard stamped washer under the head it will deform later leaving you with a loose bolt. The answer is to use a Grade 8 or hardened and ground washer under the head of the SHCS bolt.

The only thing better than an SHCS is one with a button head. These little rounded heads look like rivets. The button head allows for only a very shallow female socket, meaning you can't get a good grip with the wrench. So don't use the button heads when you need serious clamping pressure.

CHROME AND STAINLESS

They say chrome is king, but there is a problem - the fact that these bolts have no marking on the head, so there is no easy way to judge their quality. For this reason it's extra important that you purchase the bolts from a supplier you trust.

You can have your own bolts chrome plated, but considering the availability of already-chromed bolts it's not a good trade off. The process can add to the dimensions of the threads creating problems later. If in doubt about any bolt or nut, it's a good idea to chase the threads with a tap or die. If the die or tap is doing much cutting, there's a problem and the best approach is to look for a replacement.

Anyone who has used any chrome plated SHCS bolts soon discovers that rust often develops down inside the head, due to the fact that the chrome plating process just can't get plating down into those crevices. The answer is to use the little chrome caps that snap into the socket, paint the inside of the heads, or put a dab of clear silicon on the end of the wrench the first time the bolt is used.

Though stainless bolts will never rust they do carry with them a couple of disadvantages. First, most are made from a 300 series stainless which means they are only equivalent to about a Grade 2 SAE bolt. The other little problem is the fact that stainless bolts tend to gall when screwed into a stainless nut.

ANTI-SEIZE AND LOCTITE

It's a very good idea to use anti-seize or a Loctite product on the threads of chrome or stainless bolts and capscrews. Either product will prevent metal to metal contact between the male and female threads. In

metal ions. In assembling motorcycles we often encounter chrome-plated and stainless bolts, which offer the Loctite no free-metal ions to aid the locking process. Which means that when using plated bolts or when screwing a bolt into aluminum it should first be treated with Loctite primer.

When using any Loctite product it's always a good idea to clean any dirty threads with Loctite's own Klean-n-Prime, or a product like Brake-Klean that leaves no residue behind.

Button-head SHCS look great but the head isn't as deep as a conventional SHCS, so the wrench doesn't go in as far. All this means the button-heads can't be tightened to the same degree as the standard SHCS.

the case of a chrome bolt, the plating can flake off and jam the bolt and nut. In the case of a stainless capscrew, it wants to gall in the stainless nut.

Speaking of Loctite products, there are at least seven different threadlockers from this well-known company, but not all are useful to motorcycle builders. What we call blue Loctite is technically a number 242 or 243. Either one is considered by the company to be, "a medium strength threadlocker for fasteners up to 3/4 inch." Number 243 has a slight advantage in that it's slightly stronger than 242, is quicker to set and is more tolerant of a little oil on the threads. Both products protect against rust and corrosion and both allow removal of the bolt or nut with hand tools and no heat.

The Red Loctites include numbers 262, 271, 272 and 277. Before reaching for the red material consider that some of these are meant for parts that will not be disassembled (number 270) while the rest of the red-tites "require heat and hand tools for disassembly" (though a lot of American V-Twin shops use 271 without any apparent disassembly troubles).

In order to work properly and form a good bond, Loctite requires an oxygen-free atmosphere and active

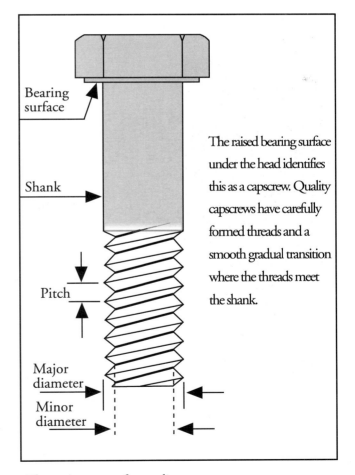

The raised bearing surface under the head identifies this as a capscrew. Quality capscrews have carefully formed threads and a smooth gradual transition where the threads meet the shank.

The major parts of a quality capscrew.

137

Chapter Eleven

Sheet Metal

Beyond Mild Customs

When you start swapping the original fenders or gas tank for something with more style, you've moved out of the realm where most of us live. No longer is this a simple "mild custom" that anyone can built in the garage at home.

For those willing to charge into these unchartered waters we present here an overview of the offerings in the sheet metal category and some basic guidelines for mounting those swoopy new shapes.

In order to move beyond the land of mild customs you have to likewise move past the use of stock sheet metal. The shapes in the catalogs can be used as is, or modified to fit your plan for the new bike.

THE METRIC MARKET

Catalogs meant for the emerging metric market aren't exactly bulging with sheet metal parts. In fact, many of the sheet metal parts that *are* available aren't metal at all. Arlen Ness offers a variety of fender shapes for metric cruisers, many in fiberglass. The shapes include the taildragger, legacy and café. In addition there are Fat-Boy type shapes from The Trike Shop and "Canadian" fenders from Bob McKay and a variety of tanks and fenders from Planet Cruiser.

Pro One makes a series of extra long and elegant fenders made from fiberglass. You can even order a pair of Indian (or should we say Drifter) fenders designed to fit the Honda ACE.

Most of these fenders come in two or more widths, which you then have to match up to the width of the fork tubes, fender struts and of course the tire itself.

Fiberglass has an advantage in that it can be easily cut so the radius of the fender better matches the radius of the wheel, or simply to trim away excess material and create a more pleasing shape.

Before buying new fenders remember you can do a lot with the stock fenders by simply replacing or eliminating trim and the stock light assemblies. This is especially true in the rear where a new light and license plate bracket can completely change the look at the back of the bike.

MOUNTING & MOCK-UP

The fenders you chose will have to fit the bike, both in a mechanical and visual sense. If you went to the trouble of

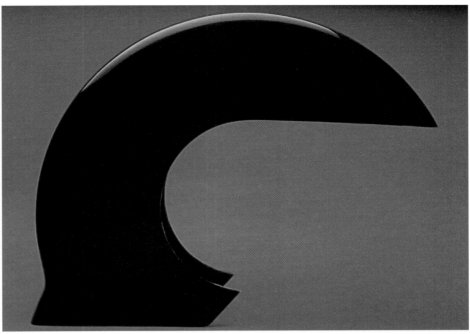

Taildragger fenders are available in various widths from Cory and Arlen Ness.

This very simple and unusual rear fender is available with an equally unusual set of fender struts. Planet Cruiser

Sportbikes meet cruisers with shapes like this aggressive rear fender from Planet Cruiser.

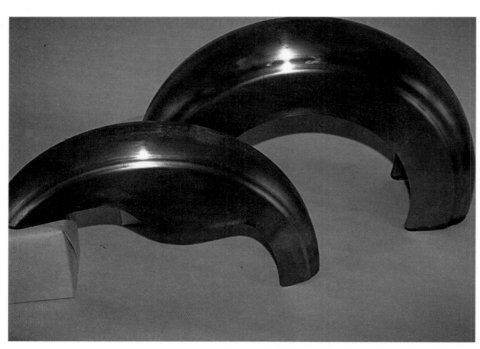

A variety of metal fenders are available in various widths and sizes from companies like Milwaukee Iron and Jesse James.

sketching up the design for the new machine as described earlier it's an excellent idea to do a complete mock-up with the bike on a hoist before sending everything out for paint. Though it sounds obvious, you have to be sure the fender radius, especially the inner radius, matches the diameter of the wheels.

You need to do the mock-up because "bolt on" parts sometimes don't, which means you need to be sure all the holes line up. Many of the fenders described above don't come with holes at all, in which case you need to clamp the parts to the bike and then figure out where to drill the holes and which fender struts to use.

The mock-up phase provides a chance to really examine the bike before you commit to painting all the parts. This exercise works better if the bike is up off the floor and you can stand back far enough to really "see" as it will look out on the street. If the rear fender you just bought doesn't look right, go borrow another one and try that. Spend time trying each part in slightly different positions, a small change in the location of a tank or fender can have a profound effect on the bike's overall appearance. All the parts need to work together and fit the look of the bike.

MOUNTING

When it comes to mounting fenders remember that the tire grows in diameter with speed. Everyone wants the fenders, especially the front one, mounted right down there one millimeter off the surface of the tire. The trouble is that street tires grow in diameter as speed increases. So what seems like enough clearance when the bike is parked in the shop might be way too little when you're running down the road at 80 plus.

Though it sounds too obvious, you have to be absolutely certain the inner fender, brackets and bolts can't possible hit the tire when the bike bottoms the suspension.

California fabricator Steve Davis told me years ago that he

likes to use button-head bolts inside the fender, installed so they point up or out, "So even if the tire does touch the bolt it isn't hitting a sharp edge that will tear the tire. People tend to ignore what might happen when the suspension bottoms hard. You need to know how the geometry works - does the tire move though an unusual arc as the suspension compresses? Can the tire hit a bolt head or trailing edge of the fender at the end of its travel. It sounds obvious, but people miss things like that all the time."

You also need to use self-locking nuts or plenty of Loctite when installing the fenders. Self-locking nylon-collar type nuts are especially handy when mounting plastic or fiberglass fenders because they provide a positive lock without the need to super-tighten the nut. To keep the wires that run inside most rear fenders out of the way, many fenders come with a small diameter piece of tubing glued into the corner of the fender. You have to be sure the tire can't reach up and touch the tube or tabs that hold the wiring harness out of harm's way.

GAS TANKS

With the exception of Planet Cruiser the metric aftermarket doesn't offer a large number of gas tank designs. Not to worry however, the Harley-Davidson market offers a wealth of gas tank designs and dimensions. Though these won't be bolt-on deals, there's a wealth of material here to draw from. The same market offers things like "tank tails" intended to make it easy to extend the length of the tank. One of the Dream Bikes seen in this book is a Intruder 1400 equipped with a modified Harley-Davidson tank that sits down over the top tube for a completely different and very pleasing look.

When mounting a gas tank it's best to stay with the mounting system intended for that tank. Many have some kind of rubber isolation system and mounts designed to properly support the considerable weight of the tank when it's full of fuel. You don't want to put stress on the mounts or brackets that hold the tank in place. If you need to have a

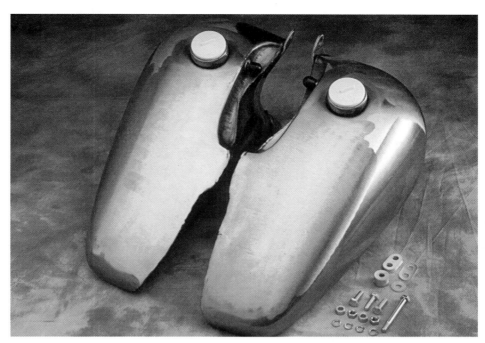

The American V-Twin catalogs are filled with gas tanks, one piece or two, with or without extensions. Mounting kits too.

new bracket welded on to the tank be sure to have the work done by a qualified welder. Poor welds are often brittle which means the weld or the area next to the weld is sure to crack later.

Many of the cruisers come to market with nifty flush-mount gas caps. For those that don't however, there are caps of this style available from the aftermarket. Though you may have to shop in an "American V-Twin" catalog, the products are there. While all of these require cutting a hole in the tank, some are bolt-in designs that can be installed without the need to do any welding. In any case be sure to match the style, vented or non-vented, to the cap that came with the tank.

When installing new sheet metal it's good to remember that the simple systems work best. By using factory brackets, fender struts and mounting systems whenever possible you save yourself work and take advantage of the tremendous R and D that Honda or Victory did in designing the brackets for that gas tank or fender. Reinventing the wheel is a lot of work.

Take to heart the comments of Steve Davis. Make sure the tire can't touch any of the mounting bolts or sharp edges. And while it's mentioned elsewhere, be sure the rear tire can't contact the stud or bolt that locates the seat.

Wolfgang Books On The Web

http://www.wolfgangpublications.com

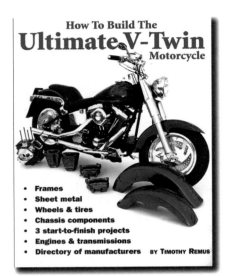

BUILD THE ULTIMATE V-TWIN MOTORCYCLE

10 chapters include:
- Build what's right for you
- Start with the right frame
- Use the best fork & suspension
- How much motor is enough
- Registration and insurance
- Paint or powder coat
- Sheet metal
- Assembly photo sequences

Ten Chapters   144 Pages

Publisher Tim Remus sought out the top custom bike builders to share their expertise with you. Hundreds of photos illustrate the extensive text. This is a revised edition with updated information and new products. If you're dreaming of the Ultimate V-Twin this is the place to start.

$19.95

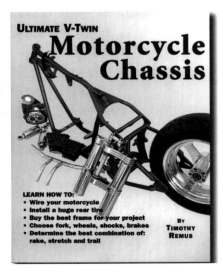

BUILD THE ULTIMATE V-TWIN CHASSIS

Ten chapters with 250+ photos.
- Frame buyers guide
- Which fork to buy
- Installing the driveline
- Sheet metal choices
- Powder coat or paint
- Mount a super wide rear tire
- How to pick the best brakes
- Understand motorcycle wiring

Ten Chapters   144 Pages

The foundation of any custom or scratch-built motorcycle is the frame. The look, ride and handling are all determined by the chassis. This book is part Buyer's Guide and part Assembly Manual. Shop Tours of Arlen Ness and M-C Specialties show how the pros do it.

$19.95

ULTIMATE SHEET METAL FABRICATION

Over 350 photos
11 chapters include:
- Layout a project
- Pick the right material
- Shrinkers & stretchers
- English wheel
- Make & use simple tooling
- Weld aluminum or steel
- Use hand and power tools

Eleven Chapters   144 Pages

In an age when most products are made by the thousands, many yearn for the one-of-kind metal creation. Whether you're building or restoring a car, motorcycle, airplane or (you get the idea), you'll find the information you need to custom build your own parts from steel or aluminum.

$19.95

More Great Books From Wolfgang Publications!

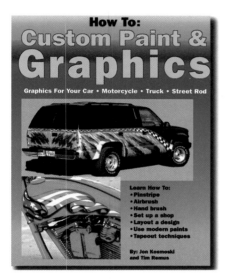

HOW TO: CUSTOM PAINT & GRAPHICS

Over 250 photos, 50% in color

7 chapters include:

- Shop tools and equipment
- Paint and materials
- Letter & pinstripe by hand
- Design and tapeouts
- Airbrushing
- Hands-on, Flames and signs
- Hands-on, Graphics

Seven Chapters   144 Pages

A joint effort of the master of custom painting, Jon Kosmoski and Tim Remus, this is the book for anyone who wants to try their hand at dressing up their street rod, truck or motorcycle with lettering, flames or exotic graphics. A great companion to Kustom Painting Secrets (below).

$24.95

KUSTOM PAINTING SECRETS

250 photos with color section

7 chapters include:

- History of House of Kolor
- How to Set up a shop
- Color painting sequences
- Prepare for paint
- Final paint application
- Hands-on, basic paint jobs
- Hands-on, beyond basic paint

Seven Chapters   128 Pages

- Hands-on, custom painting

More from the master! From the basics to advanced custom painting tricks, Jon Kosmoski shares his 30 years of experience in this book. Photos by publisher Tim Remus bring Jon's text to life. A must for ayone interested in the art of custom painting.

$19.95

BUILD THE ULTIMATE AMERICAN HOT ROD

Over 250 photos

11 chapters include:

- Planning
- Which frame to buy & why
- Suspension choices
- Brake components
- Wiring & accessories
- Horsepower: how much?
- Reproduction bodies: glass or steel

Eleven Chapters   144 Pages

Your best first step in building your very own Ultimate American Hot Rod. Publisher Tim Remus goes to the top professional builders for the inside scoop on the best products, concepts and techniques. Get your dream rod off to the right start and enjoy years of high-quality cruising.

$19.95

Sources

Aeromach
11423-B Woodside Ave
Santee, CA 92071
619 258 5443
FAX: 619 258 8515
www.aeromach.net

Arlen Ness Inc
16520 E 14th St.
San Leandro, CA 94578
408 485 4808.

Baron Custom Accessories
550 Industrial Way Suite E
Ball Brooke, CA 92028
888 278 2819

Buchanans Spoke and Rim
805 W Eighth St.
Azusa, CA 91702
626 969 4655

B Ballowe Artistry
Bert Ballowe
1315 Lakefront Dr
Dandridge TN 37725
888 285 7222
FAX 865 397 3609
BalloweArtistry.com

Cobra
4915 East Hunder
Anaheim, CA 92807
714 779 7798
cobrause.com

Custom Chrome
1 Jacqueline Court
Morgan Hill, CA 95037
408 - 778-0500
FAX: 408 778-0520

Deters Polishing
7965 Main St NE
Fridley MN 55432
763 784 6005
FAX 763 784 4269

Dr. Mudspringer
8445 Sunset Rd NE
MPLS MN 55432
612 785 2191

FDR Honda Kawasaki
1034 Broadway
Puducah, KY 42001
270 442 1655

Highway Hawk
highwayhawk.usa.com
888 449 2942

House of Kolor Paint
Valspar
210 Crosby St.
Picayune MS 39466

Jaz Cycle Service
8413 Center Drive Northeast
Spring Lake Park, MN 55432
763 792 9387

Bob McKay
271 Princess St.
Shallow Lake, Ontario NOH
2KO
Canada

Kokesh MC parts
8302 NE Hwy 65
Spring Lake Park, MN 55432
763 786 9050

Nitrous Express
4923 Lake park dr.
Wichita, Falls, TX 76302

Race Tech
3227 Producer Way #127
Pomona, CA 91768
909 594 7755
www.race-tech.com

Roadhouse Brand
60 West Easy St. No.6
Simi Valley, CA 93065
805 579 1882
www.roadhousebrand.com

Thunder Motorcycle Accessories
4210 No 39th Av
Phoenix AZ 85019-3511
602 269 5033
FAX: 602 272 5715
THUNDERMFG.COM

Planet Cruiser
2410 No Lombardy St
Richmond, VA 23220
804 329 8232
804 329 8070

Progressive Suspension
11129 G Avenue
Hesperia, CA 92345
760 948 4012

Sumax
337 Clear Rd.
Oriskany, NY 13424
315 768 1058

Wizard Custom Studios
Bruce Bush
Blaine, MN
612 792 9025

Works Shocks
21045 Osborne st
Conoga Park CA 91436
818 701 1015

Xtreme Paint Company
7731 Pillsbury Ave So
MPLS MN 55423
612 866 8222